BE MINE

An Anthology for Lovers,
Weddings and Ever After

Edited by Sally Emerson

Little, Brown

LITTLE, BROWN

First published in Great Britain as a paperback original in 2007
by Little, Brown
Reprinted 2008, 2009

Introduction and selection copyright © Sally Emerson 2007

Copyright of poems rests with authors and other rights holders as
cited in the acknowledgements on pages 263–274, which constitute an
extension of this copyright page

A CIP catalogue record for this book
is available from the British Library.

ISBN 978-0-316-73258-1

Typeset in Bembo by M Rules
Printed and bound in Great Britain by
Clays Ltd, St Ives plc

Papers used by Little, Brown are natural, renewable and recyclable
products sourced from well-managed forests and certified
in accordance with the rules of the Forest Stewardship Council.

Mixed Sources
Product group from well-managed
forests and other controlled sources
www.fsc.org   Cert no. SGS-COC-004081
© 1996 Forest Stewardship Council

FSC

Little, Brown
An imprint of
Little, Brown Book Group
100 Victoria Embankment
London EC4Y 0DY

An Hachette UK Company
www.hachette.co.uk

www.littlebrown.co.uk

To Peter

CONTENTS

FEVERS

✷

VALENTINES

✷

THORNS

𝄐

WHAT IS LOVE?

II COMMITMENT

INTIMACY

꩜

TO WED OR NOT TO WED?

꩜

PROPOSALS

III WEDDING DAY

SHARING LOVE

Sharing a Life

cℑ

IV EVER AFTER

AN INTERESTING ENTERPRISE

ℭ

LASTING LOVE

ℭ

INTRODUCTION

There are two loves. One is the passionate, desperate, wild state of being in love when the hormones dance and the skin glows. The other is the more stable, complex state of loving someone and becoming so close your roots entwine together. A wedding can be the gate between these two states.

This collection of poetry and prose is for lovers. Inside are some of the world's most beautiful love poems as well as readings, both comic and profound. I hope it will be used for weddings and valentines, wedding anniversaries and vow renewals, for ceremonies civil or religious and for civil partnerships. Above all, I hope it will be enjoyed by anyone who wants to try to understand one of our great mysteries – that of love. This anthology charts and celebrates the two stages of love: romantic, crazy love; and the profound pleasures of a long-lasting love. The Valentine poems could be spoken at a wedding service; most of the wedding poems from Sharing Love and Sharing a Life could turn up on a valentine; while many would do credit to a golden wedding anniversary. Some of the shortest are the sweetest, such as Gertrude Stein's 'A Very Valentine', which begins: 'Very fine is my valentine./Very fine and very mine.' All can be read just for pleasure.

The anthology is a journey, a boisterous ride through the storms of love – read Peggy Lee's 'Fever' – towards some kind of understanding of what makes substantial, long-lasting love and why we human beings seem to need that love. A successful wedding, after all, isn't the one where everyone has a wonderful time but the one where the couple have a wonderful time for the rest of their lives. In *Captain Corelli's Mandolin* Dr Iannis says to his daughter Pelagia: 'Love itself is what is left over when being in love has burned away, and this is both an art and a fortunate accident. Your mother and I had it, we had roots that grew towards each other underground, and when all the pretty blossom had fallen from our branches we found that we were one tree and not two.' My parents have this love. They're in their eighties, married sixty years, and still intensely love each other. My mother only has to go out shopping for a few hours for my father to clasp her on her return, declaiming, 'How could you leave me for so long?' He stares into my mother's face and looks at me in wonderment. 'Isn't she beautiful? Isn't it extraordinary that at eighty-four she doesn't have any wrinkles?' (She does.)

If marriages are about time, romance is about timelessness, that moment when the world stops and only the present exists. Read Jenny Joseph's ecstatic 'The sun has burst the sky/Because I love you' or John Donne's sublime 'The Sun Rising' or 'The Good Morrow', which revel in the bliss of being completely happy, completely present in a moment: 'Nothing else is.' A wedding is the link between the timeless rapture of romance and the reality of time and change that a marriage has to embrace. Robert Creeley wrote: 'Love comes quietly,/finally, drops/about me, on me,/in the old ways./ What did I know/thinking myself/able to go/alone all the way.'

But a great marriage makes the ordinary transcendent. It brings timelessness into the most ordinary moments, of feeding a child, laughing over a flooded floor, walking in the garden as night falls. All these are multiple strands of a lifetime together, referring back to the past and looking forward to the future, when perhaps you have become old and you walk in your garden at night, smelling the jasmine and remembering. Domestic life is repetitive, crowded with small problems and chores, but poet after poet (usually female) capture the glory of that very ordinariness and repetitiveness. U. A. Fanthorpe's 'Atlas' is about the kind of love 'which upholds/The permanently rickety elaborate/Structures of living; which is Atlas'. It is no longer a fever, but something complex, extraordinary, every bit as wonderful as first love, this weaving of a whole life, with children, houses, belonging to a chain of generations, linking family with family, creating a building that can be of astonishing strength.

Of the big three – birth, marriage, death – marriage is the only one we have much control over, so we might as well relish it, understand it, try to make it work. To marry requires great imagination, a grandeur of thought and ambition. It says yes to the world, and to a ritual, and to love. It's a brave step, certainly, but who wants to live in the safety of the shadows of life? Molly Bloom's last words in *Ulysses* are 'his heart was going like mad and yes I said yes I will Yes'. The idea of marrying is an almighty Yes, in the face of all the cynicism and negativity and hedging of bets.

The words of great writers come into their own at the major turning points of birth, marriage and death (my previous anthology, *In Loving Memory*, is to help with grief, and for memorial services, while this one is to help with love, and for weddings). We need something more than everyday words to commemorate these rites of passage, when the world turns on its axis, and nothing is the same again. Whether it is the moment when you say to your lover, yes, you will marry, or the moment of the actual marriage, when you say 'I do', you need the ritual and magic of the mightiest words available. Here are Shakespeare, Plato, Zelda Fitzgerald, Joan Didion, Homer, Stendhal, Sophocles, Emily Brontë, Margaret Atwood: their thoughts about the nature of love, all miraculous, mostly puzzled.

What I have learnt above all else from compiling this anthology (and from life) is that feverish, romantic love is reckless and dangerous, and it takes no hostages. John Lyly wrote: 'Both might and malice, deceit and treachery, all perjury, any impiety may lawfully be committed in love, which is lawless.' The lawlessness of romantic love is a reason to marry and escape all that pain, year in, year out, though even the most contented married couple might miss what the composers Rodgers and Hart call 'The sleepless nights, the daily fights . . . The fine mismating of a him and her' in their song 'I Wish I Were in Love Again'. Thomas Carlyle wrote: 'Love is not altogether a delirium, yet it has many points in common therewith.' H. L. Mencken said: 'To be in love is . . . to mistake an ordinary young man for a Greek god or an ordinary young woman for a goddess.' That, of course, is the glory as well as the danger of love.

Some of the funniest lines, useful for wedding speeches, occur in the ruminations in the section To Wed or Not to Wed. In particular, look at Darwin's scribbled notes on the pros and cons of marriage, written in two columns, in 1837 or 1838. Under the advantages of 'Not Marry' he wrote: 'Not forced to visit relatives' and 'Loss of time' but under the 'Marry' heading came 'a nice soft wife on a sofa with good fire'. He married Emma Wedgwood in January 1839. In the Proposals section we see man after man laying out his wares ('though my house be thatched, it shall go hard but I will have one half of it slated'). I like the simplicity of the anonymous American suitor: 'I feel sad when I don't see you. Be married, why won't you?'

I was surprised it was Albert Einstein (not best known for his comic asides) who said, 'Women marry men hoping they will change. Men marry women hoping they will not. So each is inevitably disappointed.' After all the torrid tales of fever and romance, read Arthur Helps' remark that 'No man, or woman, was ever cured of love by discovering the falseness of his or her lover. The living together for three long, rainy days in the country has done more to dispel love than all the perfidies in love that have ever been committed.'

Famous poems mix with lesser-known ones, verse with prose, the renowned with the anonymous, plus songs that include Sting's menacing romance 'Every Breath You Take', and Lear's cheery 'The Owl and the Pussy-Cat'.

Here also are public poems and readings, as well as private ones. The wedding ceremony, while being intimate, has a public dimension. Some of the more personal poems might seem too intense and private for a large ceremony but could be good for a small group of friends. Among the poems about intimacy, look at Margaret Atwood's 'I would like to be the air/that inhabits you for a moment/only.' Look also in Valentines where Carol Ann Duffy records how love comes 'like a sudden flight of birds/from earth to heaven after rain. Your kiss,/recalled, unstrings, like pearls, this chain of words.'

The griefs and problems of marriage are the griefs and problems of living, many and multifarious, and I have only touched on problems such as fidelity in An Interesting Enterprise. After all, this is a book for 'lovers and ever after'. In this section there are poems about change, which is the heart of a good marriage, as Wendell Berry affirmed when he wrote: 'Love changes, and in change is true.' For once Shakespeare was wrong; love is love which alters when it alteration finds.

Good marriages react, improvise, shift and develop, allow periods of loathing and of loving. I have included a poem of mine here about my marriage called 'Wrong Turnings', because anthologies are very personal, and this reveals my own feelings about marriage. In that useful cliché, it shows where I'm coming from.

The young Daisy Ashford clearly had no doubt about the point of marriage. She wrote, 'Ethel and Bernard returned from their Honymoon with a son and hair a nice fat baby called Ignatius Bernard. They soon had six more children four boys and three girls and some of them were twins which was very exciting.' The statistics suggest that those who are married with young children are less likely to split up than those who are not married and have young children. It is extraordinary that more is not done to protect and encourage the institution of marriage.

As a small child I used to worry a great deal about how exactly a person found the one man or woman in the entire world who was The One. As far as I could see there were a great deal of people in the world and The One might never come into view. He might have his head down reading a newspaper when you walked by on the Tube platform. Or he might live in Australia, say. Among the many other worries I had – such as where *exactly* was heaven? – this anxiety about The One was probably the worst. Art Garfunkel's 'Looking for the Right One' is one of the songs I've included, and if this collection guides anyone in the right direction it will have achieved its purpose.

My daughter had a different anxiety. After seeing Disney's *Snow White* she was visibly shaken.

'Was it the wicked witch that scared you?' I asked her, as she walked home beside me, clutching her pink cardigan.

She tilted her face up to me, white with horror.

'No, I liked the witch, it was the *prince* I was scared of. Poor Snow White . . . He took her away from her home.'

'No, she lived happily ever after.'

'He took her away,' my daughter repeated grimly.

Perhaps this is what the fear of marriage is, the fear of being taken away from who you really are. But sometimes it is through marriage you find that self.

I

FALLING IN LOVE

First Loves

The First Day

I wish I could remember the first day,
First hour, first moment of your meeting me;
If bright or dim the season, it might be
Summer or winter for aught I can say.
So unrecorded did it slip away,
So blind was I to see and to foresee,
So dull to mark the budding of my tree
That would not blossom yet for many a May.

If only I could recollect it! Such
A day or days! I let it come and go
As traceless as a thaw of bygone snow.
It seemed to mean so little, meant so much!
If only now I could recall that touch,
First touch of hand in hand! Did one but know!

CHRISTINA ROSSETTI (1830–94)

Like a Flame

Raising up
from my weeding
of ripening cane

my eyes
make four
with this man

there ain't
no reason
to laugh

but
I laughing
in confusion

his hands
soft his words
quick his lips
curling as in
prayer

I nod

I like this man

Tonight
I go to meet him
like a flame

GRACE NICHOLS (1950–)

Conviction (iv)

I like to get off with people,
I like to lie in their arms,
I like to be held and tightly kissed,
Safe from all alarms.

I like to laugh and be happy
With a beautiful beautiful kiss,
I tell you, in all the world
There is no bliss like this.

STEVIE SMITH (1902–71)

from Middlemarch

When Mrs Casaubon was announced he started up as from an electric shock, and felt a tingling at his finger-ends. Any one observing him would have seen a change in his complexion, in the adjustment of his facial muscles, in the vividness of his glance, which might have made them imagine that every molecule in his body had passed the message of a magic touch. And so it had. For effective magic is transcendent nature; and who shall measure the subtlety of those touches which convey the quality of soul as well as body, and make a man's passion for one woman differ from his passion for another as joy in the morning light over valley and river and white mountain-top differs from joy among Chinese lanterns and glass panels?

GEORGE ELIOT (1819–80)

Love: Beginnings

They're at that stage where so much desire streams
    between them, so much frank need and want,
so much absorption in the other and the self and the self-
    admiring entity and unity they make –
her mouth so full, breast so lifted, head thrown back so
    far in her laughter at his laughter,
he so solid, planted, oaky, firm, so resonantly factual in
    the headiness of being craved so,
she almost wreathed upon him as they intertwine again,
    touch again, cheek, lip, shoulder, brow,
every glance moving toward the sexual, every glance
    away soaring back in flame into the sexual –
that just to watch them is to feel again that hitching in
    the groin, that filling of the heart,
the old, sore heart, the battered, foundered, faithful heart,
    snorting again, stamping in its stall.

C. K. WILLIAMS (1936–)

First Love

I ne'er was struck before that hour
   With love so sudden and so sweet,
Her face it bloomed like a sweet flower
   And stole my heart away complete.
My face turned pale as deadly pale,
   My legs refused to walk away,
And when she looked, what could I ail?
   My life and all seemed turned to clay.

And then my blood rushed to my face
   And took my eyesight quite away,
The trees and bushes round the place
   Seemed midnight at noonday.
I could not see a single thing,
   Words from my eyes did start –
They spoke as chords do from the string,
   And blood burnt round my heart.

Are flowers the winter's choice?
   Is love's bed always snow?
She seemed to hear my silent voice,
   Not love's appeals to know.
I never saw so sweet a face
   As that I stood before.
My heart has left its dwelling-place
   And can return no more.

JOHN CLARE (1793–1864)

Sunday

The mint bed is in
bloom: lavender haze
day. The grass is
more than green and
throws up sharp and
cutting lights to
slice through the
plane tree leaves. And
on the cloudless blue
I scribble your name.

JAMES SCHUYLER (1923–91)

Upon Julia's Clothes

When as in silks my Julia goes,
Then, then (methinks) how sweetly flows
That liquefaction of her clothes.

Next, when I cast mine eyes and see
That brave vibration each way free;
O how that glittering taketh me!

ROBERT HERRICK (1591–1674)

The Wings of the Dove

When age chills the blood, when our
   pleasures are past –
For years flee away with the wings
   of the dove –
The dearest remembrance will still
   be the last,
Our sweetest memorial the first kiss
   of love.

LORD BYRON (1788–1824)

Years Ago

It was what we did not do that I remember,
Places with no markers left by us,
All of a summer, meeting every day,
A memorable summer of hot days,
Day after day of them, evening after evening.
Sometimes we would laze

Upon the river-bank, just touching hands
Or stroking one another's arms with grasses.
Swans floated by seeming to assert
Their dignity. But we too had our own
Decorum in the small-change of first love.

Nothing was elegiac or nostalgic,
We threw time in the river as we threw
Breadcrumbs to an inquisitive duck, and so
Day entered evening with a sweeping gesture,
Idly we talked of food and where to go.

This is the love that I knew long ago.
Before possession, passion, and betrayal.

ELIZABETH JENNINGS (1926–2001)

Passing By

There is a Lady sweet and kind,
Was never face so pleased my mind;
I did but see her passing by,
And yet I love her till I die.

Her gesture, motion, and her smiles,
Her wit, her voice, my heart beguiles.
Beguiles my heart, I know not why,
And yet I love her till I die.

Cupid is wingèd and doth range,
Her country so my love doth change:
But change she earth, or change she sky,
Yet will I love her till I die.

ANONYMOUS

The Gateway

Every marriage, every love affair, and every unhappy passion begins with the first kiss. It is the gateway to passionate love or passionate hate, to heaven or hell. The first kiss has within it the possibilities of glorious consummation, the full flowering of a lifetime love, the bitterness of final betrayal or the despair of loss.

ANONYMOUS

Looking for the Right One

Recorded by Art Garfunkel (1975)

I've been so unlucky, I'm no good at playing games
I remember their faces; forget their names.
Thought I'd found the right one, but she hasn't found me,
So I bundle up my emotions and start,
Looking for the right one.
But will the right one ever come along?
Oh, I'm looking for the right one,
When will the right one come along?
They say there's no use runnin' after something you'll never get,
But my heart says, 'Don't say no.'
Somewhere in this lonesome city is the woman for me,
But would I wait another lifetime just to keep on
Looking for the right one
But will the right one ever come along?
Oh, I'm looking for the right one,
When will the right one come along?
They say love always comes and goes,
Well, that I already know. Yes, I really know.
Looking for the right one
But will the right one ever come along?
Looking for the right one,
But will the right one come along?

STEPHEN BISHOP

from Love's Young Dream

There is nothing half so sweet in life
As love's young dream.

THOMAS MOORE (1779–1852)

from Troilus and Cressida

ACT III, SCENE II

I was won . . . With the first glance.

from Twelfth Night

ACT I, SCENE I

O Spirit of love! how quick and fresh art thou.

WILLIAM SHAKESPEARE (1564–1616)

Magic

The magic of first love is our ignorance that it can ever end.

BENJAMIN DISRAELI (1804–81)

Fevers

Fever

Sung by Peggy Lee (1958) and Madonna (1998)

Never know how much I love you,
Never know how much I care.
When you put your arms around me,
I get a Fever that's so hard to bear.

You give me Fever
When you kiss me
Fever when you hold me tight.
Fever in the morning,
Fever all through the night.

Sun lights up the day-time,
Moon lights up the night.
I light up when you call my name,
And you know I'm gonna treat you right.

You give me Fever
When you kiss me
Fever when you hold me tight.
Fever in the morning,
Fever all through the night.

Ev'rybody's got the Fever
That is something you all know
Fever isn't such a new thing
Fever started long ago.

Romeo loved Juliet
Juliet she felt the same.
When he put his arms around her, he said,
'Julie, baby you're my flame.'

Thou givest Fever, when we kisseth
Fever with thy flaming youth.
Fever – I'm afire
Fever, yea I burn forsooth.

Captain Smith and Pocahontas
Had a very mad affair
When her Daddy tried to kill him, she said,
'Daddy-o don't you dare.'

Give me Fever, with his kisses,
Fever when he holds me tight.
Fever – I'm his Missus
Oh Daddy won't you treat him right.

Now you've listened to my story
Here's the point that I have made.
Chicks were born to give you Fever
Be it fahrenheit or centigrade.

They give you Fever when you kiss them
Fever if you live and learn.
Fever – till you sizzle
What a lovely way to burn.

JOHN DAVENPORT and EDDIE COOLEY

Yearn On

I want you to feel
the unbearable lack of me.
I want your skin
to yearn for the soft lure of mine;
I want those hints of red
on your canvas
to deepen in passion for me:
carmine, burgundy.
I want you to keep
stubbing your toe
on the memory of me;
I want your head to be dizzy
and your stomach in a spin;
I want you to hear my voice
in your ear, to touch your face
imagining it is my hand.
I want your body to shiver and quiver
at the mere idea of mine.
I want you to feel as though
life after me is dull, and pointless,
and very, very aggravating;
that with me you were lifted
on a current you waited all your life to find,
and had despaired of finding
as though you were wading
through a soggy swill of inanity and ugliness
every minute we are apart.
I want you to drive yourself crazy
with the fantasy of me,
and how we will meet again, against all odds,
and there will be tears and flowers,
and the vast relief of not I,
but us.
I am haunting your dreams,

conducting these fevers
from a distance,
a distance that leaves me weeping,
and storming,
and bereft.

KATIE DONOVAN (1962–)

To Fanny Brawne, 1819

I cannot exist without you – I am forgetful of every thing but seeing
you again – my life seems to stop there – I see no further. You have
absorb'd me.

I have a sensation at the present moment as though I were
dissolving . . . I have been astonished that men could die martyrs for
religion – I have shudder'd at it – I shudder no more – I could be
martyr'd for my religion – love is my religion – I could die for that –
I could die for you. My creed is love and you are its only tenet – you
have ravish'd me away by a power I cannot resist.

JOHN KEATS (1795–1821)

26

Warming Her Pearls

Next to my own skin, her pearls. My mistress
bids me wear them, warm them, until evening
when I'll brush her hair. At six, I place them
round her cool, white throat. All day I think of her,

resting in the Yellow room, contemplating silk
or taffeta, which gown tonight? She fans herself
whilst I work willingly, my slow heat entering
each pearl. Slack on my neck, her rope.

She's beautiful. I dream about her
in my attic bed; picture her dancing
with tall men, puzzled by my faint persistent scent
beneath her French perfume, her milky stones.

I dust her shoulders with a rabbit's foot,
watch the soft blush seep through her skin
like an indolent sigh. In her looking-glass
my red lips part as though I want to speak.

Full moon. Her carriage brings her home. I see
her every movement in my head . . . Undressing,
taking off her jewels, her slim hand reaching
for the case, slipping naked into bed, the way

she always does . . . And I lie here awake,
knowing the pearls are cooling even now
in the room where my mistress sleeps. All night
I feel their absence and I burn.

CAROL ANN DUFFY (1955–)

Temptation

Call yourself alive? Look, I promise you
that for the first time you'll feel your pores opening
like fish mouths, and you'll actually be able to hear
your blood surging through all those lanes,
and you'll feel light gliding across the cornea
like the train of a dress. For the first time
you'll be aware of gravity
like a thorn in your heel,
and your shoulder blades will ache for want of wings.
Call yourself alive? I promise you
you'll be deafened by dust falling on the furniture,
you'll feel your eyebrows turning to two gashes,
and every memory you have – will begin
at Genesis.

NINA CASSIAN (1924–)

Jewels

My love was nude, but, knowing my desire,
Had donned her sounding jewels, an attire
That, with its air of triumph rich and brave,
Recalled some sultan's proud and favoured slave.

That radiant world of gem and metal dancing
Strikes forth a music mocking and entrancing;
I love it madly, for my chief delight
Is in the interplay of sound and light.

She lay there, then, and let herself be loved,
And from her couch she smiled down and approved
My deep, calm love that rose to her as if
It were an ocean mounting to a cliff.

Eyeing me like a well-tamed tigress there,
She posed with a distracted dreamy air,
And candour joined to lewdness lent a new
Strange charm to metamorphoses I knew.

Her oil-bright, swan-like arms, legs, loins and thighs,
All undulating, passed before my eyes
Clairvoyant and serene; those fruits of mine,
Her belly and breasts, the cluster on my vine,

Advanced like evil angels to cajole
And trouble the quiescence of my soul,
Dislodging her from the crystal rock where she
In solitude was resting peacefully.

She so thrust out her pelvis that it seemed
She made Antiope's plump hips combine
With the smooth bust of a youth in a new design.
On her tawny skin rouge exquisitely gleamed.

– And as the dead lamp left us half in gloom,
And now the hearth alone lit up the room,
With every flaming sigh there came a flood
Of light that drowned her amber skin in blood.

CHARLES BAUDELAIRE (1821–67)

To Josephine Beauharnais, 1795

I wake filled with thoughts of you. Your portrait and the intoxicating evening which we spent yesterday have left my senses in turmoil. Sweet, incomparable Josephine, what a strange effect you have on my heart! Are you angry? Do I see you looking sad? Are you worried? . . . My soul aches with sorrow, and there can be no rest for your lover; but is there still more in store for me when, yielding to the profound feelings which overwhelm me, I draw from your lips, from your heart a love which consumes me with fire? Ah! it was last night that I fully realised how false an image of you your portrait gives!

You are leaving at noon; I shall see you in three hours.

Until then, *mio dolce amor*, a thousand kisses; but give me none in return, for they set my blood on fire.

NAPOLEON BONAPARTE (1769–1821)

To Mary Scurlock, 1707

Madam,

It is the hardest thing in the world to be in love and yet attend to business. As for me, all who speak to me find me out, and I must lock myself up or other people will do it for me.

A gentleman asked me this morning, 'What news from Lisbon?' and I answered, 'She is exquisitely handsome.' Another desired to know when I had been last at Hampton Court. I replied, 'It will be on Tuesday come se'nnight. Prythee, allow me at least to kiss your hand before that day, that my mind may be in some composure.' O love! —

> A thousand torments dwell about me!
> Yet who would live to live without thee?

Methinks I could write a volume to you; but all the language on earth would fail in saying how much and with what disinterested passion I am ever yours.

RICHARD STEELE (1672–1729)

My Love is Like to Ice

My love is like to ice, and I to fire:
How comes it then that this her cold so great
Is not dissolved through my so hot desire,
But harder grows the more I her entreat?
Or how comes it that my exceeding heat
Is not allayed by her heart-frozen cold,
But that I burn much more in boiling sweat,
And feel my flames augmented manifold?
What more miraculous thing may be told,
That fire, which all things melts, should harden ice,
And ice, which is congealed with senseless cold,
Should kindle fire by wonderful device?
Such is the power of love in gentle mind,
That it can alter all the course of kind.

EDMUND SPENSER (c. 1552–99)

Wild Nights! Wild Nights!

Wild nights! Wild nights!
Were I with thee,
Wild nights should be
Our luxury!

Futile the winds
To a heart in port, –
Done with the compass,
Done with the chart.

Rowing in Eden!
Ah! the sea!
Might I but moor
To-night in thee!

EMILY DICKINSON (1830–86)

To Evelina Hanska, 1833

To you, my love, a thousand tendernesses. Yesterday, I have been rushing about the whole day; I found myself so fatigued that I allowed myself to sleep all night, and then I made a mental prayer to my idol. I went to sleep in sweet thoughts of you, as, if married, I should have slept in the arms of my well-beloved. Good heavens; I am terrified to see how much my life is yours. With what rapidity it rushes towards your heart. Your arteries beat as much for me as for yourself. Adored darling, how much good your letters do me. I believe in you, you see, as I believe in my respiration. I am with regard to this bliss like a child, like a man of science, like a fool taking care of tulips. I weep with rage at not being near you. I collect all my ideas in order to develop this love, and I am here watching incessantly for it to increase without obstructions. Is there not something in this of the child, the man of science, and the botanist? . . .

I must, my angel, resume my drudgery; but it will not be without having laid before you here all the flowers of my heart, a thousand tendernesses, a thousand caresses, all the vows of a poor solitary who lives between his thoughts and his love.

Goodbye, my cherished beauty; one kiss on those beautiful red lips, so fresh, so tender, a kiss which goes far, which encompasses you. I do not say goodbye to you. Oh! When shall I have your dear portrait? If you happen to get it mounted, let it be kept between two enamel plates and let the whole of it not be thicker than a five-franc piece, for I wish to wear it always over my heart. It will be my talisman; I shall feel it there; I shall gather strength and courage from it. From it will dart forth the rays of that fame which I want to be so great, so wide, so radiant, to envelope you in its light.

Well I must quit you, always with regret. But once free and without worries, what sweet pilgrimage. This is the reason why I work so hard. Ah, God! how happy the rich are. They travel post haste and fly like swallows. But my thought travels more quickly, and every night it creeps around your heart, it covers you.

HONORÉ DE BALZAC (1799–1850)

34

Sonnet 147

My love is as a fever, longing still
For that which longer nurseth the disease,
Feeding on that which doth preserve the ill,
Th'uncertain sickly appetite to please:
My reason, the physician to my love,
Angry that his prescriptions are not kept,
Hath left me, and I, desperate, now approve
Desire is death, which physic did except.
Past cure I am, now reason is past care,
And frantic mad with ever more unrest;
My thoughts and my discourse as madmen's are,
At random from the truth vainly expressed:
    For I have sworn thee fair, and thought thee bright,
    Who art as black as hell, as dark as night.

WILLIAM SHAKESPEARE (1564–1616)

To Be in Love

To be in love is merely to be in a state of perpetual anesthesia – to mistake an ordinary young man for a Greek god or an ordinary young woman for a goddess.

H. L. MENCKEN (1880–1956)

Indiscretion

A lover without indiscretion is not a lover at all.

THOMAS HARDY (1840–1928)

Bred by Desire

A heat full of coldness, a sweet full of bitterness, a pain full of pleasantness, which maketh thoughts have eyes, and hearts, and ears; bred by desire, nursed by delight, weaned by jealousy, killed by dissembling, buried by ingratitude and this is love.

JOHN LYLY (1554–1606)

from Tyrannic Love

Pains of love be sweeter far
Than all other pleasures are.

JOHN DRYDEN (1631–1700)

from The Rover

One hour of right-down love
Is worth an age of dully living on.

APHRA BEHN (1640–89)

New Passion

When the heart is still agitated by the remains of a passion, we are
more ready to receive a new one than when we are entirely cured.

LA ROCHEFOUCAULD (1613–80)

from Pendennis

It is best to love wisely, no doubt: but to love foolishly is better than
not to be able to love at all.

WILLIAM MAKEPEACE THACKERAY (1811–63)

Madness

Love that is not madness is not love.

PEDRO CALDERÓN (1600–81)

Heaven and Hell

O what a heaven is love! O what a hell!

THOMAS DEKKER (1570–1632)

Delirium

Love is not altogether a delirium, yet it has many points in common therewith.

THOMAS CARLYLE (1795–1881)

Odi et Amo

I hate and love. And if you ask me why
I do not know: I only feel it, and it is agony.

CATULLUS (*c.* 84–*c.* 54 BC)

Valentines

Valentine

My heart has made its mind up
And I'm afraid it's you.
Whatever you've got lined up,
My heart has made its mind up
And if you can't be signed up
This year, next year will do.
My heart has made its mind up
And I'm afraid it's you.

WENDY COPE (1945–)

To Lesbia

Let us live, my Lesbia, and let us love,
and let us judge all the rumours of old men
to be worth just one penny!
The suns are able to fall and rise:
When that brief light has fallen for us,
we must sleep a never ending night.
Give me a thousand kisses, then another hundred,
then another thousand, then a second hundred,
then yet another thousand more, then another hundred.
Then, when we have made many thousands,
we will mix them all up so that we don't know,
and so that no one can be jealous of us when he finds out
how many kisses we have shared.

CATULLUS (c. 84–c. 54 BC)
(Trans. Ben Jonson 1572–1637)

The Sun Has Burst the Sky

The sun has burst the sky
Because I love you
And the river its banks.

The sea laps the great rocks
Because I love you
And takes no heed of the moon dragging it away
And saying coldly 'Constancy is not for you.'

The blackbird fills the air
Because I love you
With spring and lawns and shadows falling on lawns.

The people walk in the street and laugh
I love you
And far down the river ships sound their hooters
Crazy with joy because I love you.

JENNY JOSEPH (1932–)

A Very Valentine

Very fine is my valentine.
Very fine and very mine.
Very mine is my valentine very mine and very fine.
Very fine is my valentine and mine, very fine very mine and
  mine is my valentine.

GERTRUDE STEIN (1874–1946)

Rapture

Thought of by you all day, I think of you.
The birds sing in the shelter of a tree.
Above the prayer of rain, unacred blue,
not paradise, goes nowhere endlessly.
How does it happen that our lives can drift
far from our selves, while we stay trapped in time,
queuing for death? It seems nothing will shift
the pattern of our days, alter the rhyme
we make with loss to assonance with bliss.
Then love comes, like a sudden flight of birds
from earth to heaven after rain. Your kiss,
recalled, unstrings, like pearls, this chain of words.
Huge skies connect us, joining here to there.
Desire and passion on the thinking air.

Carol Ann Duffy (1955–)

Her Face

Her face	Her tongue	Her wit
so fair	so sweet	so sharp
first bent	then drew	then hit
mine eye	mine ear	my heart
Mine eye	Mine ear	My heart
to like	to learn	to love
her face	her tongue	her wit
doth lead	doth teach	doth move
Her face	Her tongue	Her wit
with beams	with sound	with art
doth blind	doth charm	doth knit
mine eye	mine ear	my heart
Mine eye	Mine ear	My heart
with life	with hope	with skill
her face	her tongue	her wit
doth feed	doth feast	doth fill
O face	O tongue	O wit
with frowns	with checks	with smart
wrong not	vex not	wound not
mine eye	mine ear	my heart
This eye	This ear	This heart
shall joy	shall yield	shall swear
her face	her tongue	her wit
to serve	to trust	to fear.

ARTHUR GORGES (1557–1625)

Alicante

An orange on the table
Your dress on the rug
And you in my bed
Sweet present of the present
Cool of night
Warmth of my life.

JACQUES PRÉVERT (1900–77)
(Trans. Lawrence Ferlinghetti 1920–)

My True Love Hath My Heart and I Have His

My true love hath my heart and I have his,
By just exchange one for the other given.
I hold his dear, and mine he cannot miss,
There never was a better bargain driven.
    My true love hath my heart and I have his.

His heart in me keeps me and him in one,
My heart in him his thoughts and senses guides:
He loves my heart, for once it was his own,
I cherish his because in me it bides
    My true love hath my heart, and I have his.

SIR PHILIP SIDNEY (1554–86)

Valentine

The things about you I appreciate
    May seem indelicate:
I'd like to find you in the shower
And chase the soap for half an hour.
I'd like to have you in my power
    And see your eyes dilate.
I'd like to have your back to scour
And other parts to lubricate.
Sometimes I feel it is my fate
To chase you screaming up a tower
    Or make you cower
By asking you to differentiate
    Nietzsche from Schopenhauer.
I'd like successfully to guess your weight
    And win you at a fête.
I'd like to offer you a flower.

I like the hair upon your shoulders,
Falling like water over boulders.
I like the shoulders, too: they are essential.
Your collar-bones have great potential
(I'd like all your particulars in folders
    Marked *Confidential*).

I like your cheeks, I like your nose,
I like the way your lips disclose
The neat arrangement of your teeth
(Half above and half beneath)
    In rows.

I like your eyes, I like their fringes.
The way they focus on me gives me twinges.
Your upper arms drive me berserk.
I like the way your elbows work,
    On hinges.

I like your wrists, I like your glands,
I like the fingers on your hands.
I'd like to teach them how to count,
And certain things we might exchange,
Something familiar for something strange,
I'd like to give you just the right amount
     And get some change.

I like it when you tilt your cheek up.
I like the way you nod and hold a teacup.
I like your legs when you unwind them.
Even in trousers I don't mind them.
I like each softly-moulded kneecap.
I like the little crease behind them.
I'd always know, without a recap,
     Where to find them.

I like the sculpture of your ears.
I like the way your profile disappears
Whenever you decide to turn and face me.
I'd like to cross two hemispheres
     And have you chase me.
I'd like to smuggle you across frontiers
Or sail with you at night into Tangiers.
     I'd like you to embrace me.

I'd like to see you ironing your skirt
     And cancelling other dates,
I'd like to button up your shirt.
I like the way your chest inflates.
I'd like to soothe you when you're hurt
Or frightened senseless by invert-
     ebrates.

I'd like you even if you were malign
And had a yen for sudden homicide.
I'd let you put insecticide

Into my wine.
I'd even like you if you were the Bride
     Of Frankenstein
Or something ghoulish out of Mamoulian's
     Jekyll and Hyde.
I'd even like you as my Julian
Of Norwich or Cathleen ní Houlihan.
     How melodramatic
If you were something muttering in attics
Like Mrs Rochester or a student of Boolean
     Mathematics.

You are the end of self-abuse
You are the eternal feminine.
I'd like to find a good excuse
To call on you and find you in.
I'd like to put my hand beneath your chin.
     And see you grin.
I'd like to taste your Charlotte Russe,
I'd like to feel my lips upon your skin,
I'd like to make you reproduce.

I'd like you in my confidence.
I'd like to be your second look.
I'd like to let you try the French Defence
     And mate you with my rook.
I'd like to be your preference
     And hence
I'd like to be around when you unhook.
I'd like to be your only audience,
The final name in your appointment book,
     Your future tense.

JOHN FULLER (1937–)

Strawberries

There were never strawberries
like the ones we had
that sultry afternoon
sitting on the step
of the open french window
facing each other
your knees held in mine
the blue plates in our laps
the strawberries glistening
in the hot sunlight
we dipped them in sugar
looking at each other
not hurrying the feast
for one to come
the empty plates
laid on the stone together
with the two forks crossed
and I bent towards you
sweet in that air
in my arms
abandoned like a child
from your eager mouth
the taste of strawberries
in my memory
lean back again
let me love you
let the sun beat
on our forgetfulness
one hour of all
the heat intense
and summer lightning
on the Kilpatrick hills

let the storm wash the plates.

EDWIN MORGAN (1920–)

Celia, Celia

When I am sad and weary
When I think all hope is gone
When I walk along High Holborn
I think of you with nothing on.

ADRIAN MITCHELL (1932–)

from To Mary

I sleep with thee, and wake with thee,
And yet thou art not there;
I fill my arms with thoughts of thee,
And press the common air.
Thy eyes are gazing upon mine,
When thou art out of sight;
My lips are always touching thine,
At morning, noon, and night.

JOHN CLARE (1793–1864)

Love's Philosophy

The fountains mingle with the river,
    And the rivers with the ocean;
The winds of heaven mix forever,
    With a sweet emotion;
Nothing in the word is single;
    All things by a law divine
In one another's being mingle –
    Why not I with thine?

See! the mountains kiss high heaven,
    And the waves clasp one another;
Now sister flower would be forgiven
    If it disdained its brother;
And the sunlight clasps the earth,
    And the moonbeams kiss the sea –
What are all these kissings worth,
    If thou kiss not me?

PERCY BYSSHE SHELLEY (1792–1822)

Meeting at Night

I

The grey sea and the long black land;
And the yellow half-moon large and low;
And the startled little waves that leap
In fiery ringlets from their sleep,
As I gain the cove with pushing prow,
And quench its speed i' the slushy sand.

II

Then a mile of warm sea-scented beach;
Three fields to cross till a farm appears;
A tap at the pane, the quick sharp scratch
And blue spurt of a lighted match,
And a voice less loud, thro' its joys and fears,
Than the two hearts beating each to each!

ROBERT BROWNING (1812–89)

from Romeo and Juliet

ACT II, SCENE II

JULIET: Good-night, good-night! as sweet repose and rest
Come to thy heart as that within my breast!

ROMEO: O! wilt thou leave me so unsatisfied?

JULIET: What satisfaction canst thou have tonight?

ROMEO: The exchange of thy love's faithful vow for mine.

JULIET: I gave thee mine before thou didst request it;
And yet I would it were to give again.

ROMEO: Wouldst thou withdraw it? for what purpose, love?

JULIET: But to be frank, and give it thee again.
And yet I wish but for the thing I have:
My bounty is as boundless as the sea,
My love as deep; the more I give to thee,
The more I have, for both are infinite.

WILLIAM SHAKESPEARE (1564–1616)

To Lord Alfred Douglas, *c.* 1891

My own dear boy – Your sonnet is quite lovely and it is a marvel that those red roseleaf lips of yours should be made no less for the music of song than for the madness of kissing. Your slim gilt soul walks between passion and poetry. I know that Hyacinthus, whom Apollo loved so madly, was you in Greek days. Why are you alone in London, and when do you go to Salisbury? Do go there and cool your hands in the grey twilight of Gothic things, and come here whenever you like. It is a lovely place; it only lacks you, but to Salisbury first. Always with undying love,

Yours,
Oscar

OSCAR WILDE (1854–1900)

If you were coming in the fall

If you were coming in the fall,
I'd brush the summer by
With half a smile and half a spurn,
As housewives do a fly.

If I could see you in a year,
I'd wind the months in balls,
And put them each in separate drawers,
Until their time befalls.

If only centuries delayed,
I'd count them on my hand,
Subtracting till my fingers dropped
Into Van Diemen's land.

If certain, when this life was out,
That yours and mine should be,
I'd toss it yonder like a rind,
And taste eternity.

But now, all ignorant of the length
Of time's uncertain wing,
It goads me, like the goblin bee,
That will not state its sting.

EMILY DICKINSON (1830–86)

The Sun Rising

Busy old fool, unruly Sun,
   Why dost thou thus,
Through windows, and through curtains call on us?
Must to thy motions lovers' seasons run?
    Saucy pedantic wretch, go chide
    Late school-boys, and sour 'prentices,
   Go tell court-huntsmen that the King will ride,
   Call country ants to harvest offices;
Love, all alike, no season knows, nor clime,
Nor hours, days, months, which are the rags of time.

    Thy beams, so reverend, and strong
    Why shouldst thou think?
I could eclipse and cloud them with a wink,
But that I would not lose her sight so long:
    If her eyes have not blinded thine,
    Look, and tomorrow late, tell me,
   Whether both the Indias of spice and mine
   Be where thou left'st them, or lie here with me.
Ask for those kings whom thou saw'st yesterday,
And thou shalt hear, 'All here in one bed lay.'

    She is all States, and all Princes, I;
    Nothing else is.
Princes do but play us; compar'd to this,
All honour's mimic; all wealth alchemy.
    Thou Sun an half as happy as we,
    In that the world's contracted thus;
   Thine age asks ease, and since thy duties be
   To warm the world, that's done in warming us.
Shine here to us, and thou art every where;
This bed thy centre is, these walls, thy sphere.

JOHN DONNE (1572–1631)

As Sweet

It's all because we're so alike –
Twin souls, we two.
We smile at the expression, yes,
And know it's true.

I told the shrink. He gave our love
A different name.
But he can call it what he likes –
It's still the same.

I long to see you, hear your voice,
My narcissistic object-choice.

WENDY COPE (1945–)

Fear Not to Swear

Fear not to swear; the winds carry the perjuries of lovers without effect over land and sea, thanks to Jupiter. The father of the gods himself has denied effect to what foolish lovers in their eagerness have sworn.

TIBULLUS (*c.*55–19 BC)

Love Magnifies

There are no little events with the heart. It magnifies everything; it places in the same scales the fall of an empire of fourteen years and the dropping of a woman's glove, and almost always the glove weighs more than the empire.,

HONORÉ DE BALZAC (1799–1850)

Absence

Love reckons hours for months, and days for years; and every little absence is an age.

JOHN DRYDEN (1631–1700)

from The Great Gatsby

Then wear the gold hat, if that will move her;
  If you can bounce high, bounce for her too,
Till she cry 'Lover, gold-hatted, high-bouncing lover,
  I must have you!'

THOMAS PARKE D'INVILLIERS
(alias F. Scott Fitzgerald, 1896–1940)

Thorns

from Romeo and Juliet

Is love a tender thing? It is too rough,
Too rude, too boisterous, and it pricks like thorn.

WILLIAM SHAKESPEARE (1564–1616)

Symptoms of Love

Love is a universal migraine,
A bright stain on the vision
Blotting out reason.

Symptoms of true love
Are leanness, jealousy,
Laggard dawns;

Are omens and nightmares –
Listening for a knock,
Waiting for a sign:

For a touch of her fingers
In a darkened room,
For a searching look.

Take courage, lover!
Can you endure such grief
At any hand but hers?

ROBERT GRAVES (1895–1985)

Every Breath You Take

Recorded by The Police (1983), and by Puff Daddy (1997)
as 'I'll Be Missing You'

Every breath you take,
Every move you make,
Every bond you break,
Every step you take,
I'll be watching you.

Every single day,
Every word you say,
Every game you play,
Every night you stay,
I'll be watching you.

Oh, can't you see
You belong to me
How my poor heart aches
With every step you take.

Every move you make,
Every vow you break,
Every smile you fake,
Every claim you stake,
I'll be watching you.

Since you've gone, I've been lost without a trace,
I dream at night I can only see your face,
I look around but it's you I can't replace,
I feel so cold I long for your embrace,
I keep crying baby, baby please.

Oh, can't you see
You belong to me
How my poor heart aches
With every step you take.

Every move you make,
Every vow you break,
Every smile you fake,
Every claim you stake,
I'll be watching you.

Every move you make,
Every step you take,
I'll be watching you,
I'll be watching
You

STING (1951–)

from Why Doesn't She Come?

Why doesn't she come?
  I know we said eight.
Or was it half-past?
That clock must be fast.
Why doesn't she come?
  She's ten minutes late.
I'll sit by the door
  And see her come in;
I've brought her a rose,
  I've borrowed a pin.
I'll be very severe,
I'll tell her, 'My dear,
You mustn't be late.'
It's a quarter past eight.
  Why doesn't she come?

Why doesn't she come?
  This must be the place.
She couldn't forget,
Or is she upset?
Why doesn't she come?
  Am I in disgrace?
Oh, well, if it's that,
We were both in the wrong –
I'll give her the rose
And say I was wrong.
I'll give her a kiss
And tell her I'm sorry –
'I'm *terribly* sorry . . .'
Why doesn't she come?

Perhaps she is ill –
I fancied last night
Her eyes were too bright –

68

A feverish chill?
She's lying in bed,
She's light in the head!
She's dying – she's *dead*!
  Why doesn't she come?

  Why doesn't she come?
Why doesn't she come?
It's nearly half-past.
Well, never again!
I'll send her the rose,
I won't say a word,
Just send her the rose –
She'd *laugh*, I suppose!
A flirt and a fraud!
I'll travel abroad,
I'll go to the East,
I'll shoot a wild beast.
And now for a drink,
I'll have a stiff drink –
A brandy, I think –
  And drown myself in it.
I'll shoot myself . . . Oh,
How I love her! – 'Hul-*lo*!
  What? *Late?* Not a minute!'

A. P. HERBERT (1890–1971)

Another Love

It is in vain, this silence I must break;
The fault of him I love moves me to speak.
Dearer than all the world he is to me;
But he regards not love nor courtesy,
Nor wisdom, nor my worth, nor all my beauty –
He has deceived me. Such my fate should be,
If I had failed to him in loving duty.

Oh, strange and past belief that in disdain
Your heart, oh friend, should look upon my pain;
That now another love should conquer you,
For all that I may say, that I may do!
Have you forgotten the sweet first communion
Of our two hearts? Now sorely would I rue
If by my guilt were caused this last disunion.

The noble worth, the valour you possess,
Your fame and beauty add to my distress.
For far and near the noble ladies all,
If love can move them, listen to your call.
But you, my friend, whose soul is keenest-sighted,
Must know who loves you, and is true withal.
And ah! remember now the troth we plighted.

BEATRICE DE DIE (mid-twelfth century female troubadour)

The Forsaken Lover

They flee from me that sometime did me seek
With naked foot stalking in my chamber.
I have seen them gentle, tame and meek
That now are wild, and do not remember
That sometime they put themself in danger
To take bread at my hand; and now they range,
Busily seeking with a continual change.

Thanked be fortune, it hath been otherwise
Twenty times better, but once in special:
In thin array after a pleasant guise
When her loose gown from her shoulders did fall

And she me caught in her arms long and small
Therewithal sweetly did me kiss,
And softly said, 'Dear heart, how like you this?'

It was no dream. I lay broad waking.
But all is turned through my gentleness
Into a strange fashion of forsaking,
And I have leave to go, of her goodness,
And she also to use newfangleness.
But since that I so kindly am served,
I would fain know what she hath deserved.

SIR THOMAS WYATT (1503–42)

A Love Poem

He made no promise –
so I try to tell myself
not to be bitter
until this long night too
ends with a lonely dawn.

Unrequited Love

If even now
in the midst of rejection
I still love him so,
then what would be my feelings
if he were to love me back?

Empress Eifuku (1271–1342)

Love

Two thousand cigarettes.
A hundred miles
from wall to wall.
An eternity and a half of vigils
blanker than snow.

Tons of words
old as the tracks
of a platypus in the sand.

A hundred books we didn't write.
A hundred pyramids we didn't build.

Sweepings.
Dust.

Bitter
as the beginning of the world.

Believe me when I say
it was beautiful

MIROSLAV HOLUB (1923–98)

I Wish I Were in Love Again

from the musical Babes in Arms, 1937

The sleepless nights, the daily fights,
The quick toboggan when you reach the heights;
I miss the kisses and I miss the bites,
I wish I were in love again!

The broken dates, the endless waits,
The lovely loving and the hateful hates,
The conversation with the flying plates,
I wish I were in love again!

No more pain, no more strain,
Now I'm sane, but I would rather be ga-ga!

The pulled out fur of cat and cur,
The fine mismating of a him and her,
I've learned my lesson,
But I wish I were in love again!

The furtive sigh, the blackened eye,
The words 'I'll love you till the day I die',
The self-deception that believes the lie,
I wish I were in love again!

When love congeals it soon reveals
The faint aroma of performing seals,
The double crossing of a pair of heels
I wish I were in love again!

No more care, no despair.
I'm all there now, but I'd rather be punch-drunk!

Believe me, sir, I much prefer
The classic battle of a him and her,
I don't like quiet and
I wish I were in love again!

LORENZ HART (1895–1943)

To Love is to Suffer

To love is to suffer. To avoid suffering one must not love. But then
one suffers from not loving. Therefore, to love is to suffer; not to love
is to suffer; to suffer is to suffer. To be happy is to love. To be happy,
then, is to suffer, but suffering makes one unhappy. Therefore, to be
happy one must love or love to suffer or suffer from too much
happiness.

WOODY ALLEN (1935–)

Under the Influence

When two people are under the influence of the most violent, most insane, most delusive, and most transient of passions, they are required to swear that they will remain in that excited, abnormal, and exhausting condition continuously until death do them part.

GEORGE BERNARD SHAW (1856–1950)

Desire

There is nothing like desire for preventing the thing one says from bearing any resemblance to what one has in mind.

MARCEL PROUST (1871–1922)

Rainy Days

No man, or woman, was ever cured of love by discovering the falseness of his or her lover. The living together for three long, rainy days in the country has done more to dispel love than all the perfidies in love that have ever been committed.

ARTHUR HELPS (1813–75)

Tyrant Love

O tyrant love, when held by you,
We may to prudence bid adieu.

JEAN DE LA FONTAINE (1621–95)

Lawless Love

Both might and malice, deceit and treachery, all perjury, any impiety may lawfully be committed in love, which is lawless.

JOHN LYLY (1554–1606)

Love Like You've Never Been Hurt

As we grow up, we learn that even the one person that wasn't supposed ever to let you down probably will. You will have your heart broken probably more than once and it's harder every time. You'll break hearts too, so remember how it felt when yours was broken. You'll fight with your best friend. You'll blame a new love for things an old one did. You'll cry because time is passing too fast, and you'll eventually lose someone you love. So take too many pictures, laugh too much, and love like you've never been hurt . . . Don't be afraid that your life will end, be afraid that it will never begin.

ANONYMOUS

All's Fair

All's fair in love and war.

FRANCIS EDWARD SMEDLEY (1818–64)

from Romeo and Juliet

Love is a smoke roused with the fume of sighs;
Being purged, a fire sparkling in lovers' eyes;
Being vexed, a sea nourished with lovers' tears;
What is it else? A madness most discreet,
A choking gall, and a preserving sweet.

WILLIAM SHAKESPEARE (1564–1616)

What Is Love?

Some say that love's a little boy

Some say that love's a little boy,
    And some say it's a bird,
Some say it makes the world go round,
    And some say that's absurd.
And when I asked the man next-door,
    Who looked as if he knew,
His wife got very cross indeed,
    And said it wouldn't do.

Does it look like a pair of pyjamas,
    Or the ham in a temperance hotel?
Does its odour remind one of llamas,
    Or has it a comforting smell?
Is it prickly to touch as a hedge is,
    Or soft as eiderdown fluff?
Is it sharp or quite smooth at the edges?
    O tell me the truth about love.

Our history books refer to it
    In cryptic little notes,
It's quite a common topic on
    The Transatlantic boats;
I've found the subject mentioned in
    Accounts of suicides,
And even seen it scribbled on
    The backs of railway-guides.

Does it howl like a hungry Alsatian,
    Or boom like a military band?
Could one give a first-rate imitation
    On a saw or a Steinway Grand?
Is its singing at parties a riot?
    Does it only like Classical stuff?

Will it stop when one wants to be quiet?
O tell me the truth about love.

I looked inside the summer-house;
It wasn't ever there:
I tried the Thames at Maidenhead,
And Brighton's bracing air.
I don't know what the blackbird sang,
Or what the tulip said;
But it wasn't in the chicken-run,
Or underneath the bed.

Can it pull extraordinary faces?
Is it usually sick on a swing?
Does it spend all its time at the races,
Or fiddling with pieces of string?
Has it views of its own about money?
Does it think Patriotism enough?
Are its stories vulgar but funny?
O tell me the truth about love.

When it comes, will it come without warning
Just as I'm picking my nose?
Will it knock on my door in the morning,
Or tread in the bus on my toes?
Will it come like a change in the weather?
Will its greeting be courteous or rough?
Will it alter my life altogether?
O tell me the truth about love.

W. H. AUDEN (1907–73)

from Among the Multitude

Among the men and women the multitude,
I perceive one picking me out by secret
   and divine signs
Acknowledging none else, not parent, wife,
   husband, brother, child, any nearer than
   I am
Some are baffled, but that one is not –
   that one knows me.

WALT WHITMAN (1819–92)

from The Symposium

THE DESIRE AND PURSUIT

So ancient is the desire of one another which is implanted in us, reuniting our original nature, seeking to make one of two and to heal the state of man. Each of us when separated, having one side only, like a flat fish, is but the tally-half of a man, and he is always looking for his other half . . . There is not a man . . . who would not acknowledge that this meeting and melting into one another, this becoming one instead of two, was the very expression of his ancient need. And the reason is that human nature was originally one and we were a whole, and the desire and pursuit of the whole is called Love.

PLATO (*c.* 429–347 BC)

The Power of Love

It can alter things:
The stormy scowl can become
Suddenly a smile.

The knuckly bunched fist
May open like a flower,
Tender a caress.

Beneath its bright warmth
Black ice of suspicion melts;
Danger is dazzled.

A plain and dull face
Astounds with its radiance
And sudden beauty.

Ordinary things –
Teacups, spoons and sugar-lumps –
Become magical.

The locked door opens;
Inside are leaves and moonlight;
You are welcomed in.

Its delicate strength
Can lift the heaviest heart
And snap hostile steel.

It gives eloquence
To the dumb tongue, makes plain speech
Blaze like poetry.

VERNON SCANNELL (1922–)

In a Bath Teashop

'Let us not speak, for the love we bear one another
    Let us hold hands and look.'
She, such a very ordinary little woman;
    He, such a thumping crook;
But both, for a moment, little lower than the angels
    In the teashop's ingle-nook.

JOHN BETJEMAN (1906–84)

from The Prophet

Love has no other desire but to fulfil itself.
But if you love and must needs have desires, let
    these be your desires:
To melt and be like a running brook that sings its
    melody to the night.
To know the pain of too much tenderness.
To be wounded by your own understanding of love;
And to bleed willingly and joyfully.
To wake at dawn with a winged heart and give
    thanks for another day of loving;
To rest at the noon hour and meditate love's ecstasy;
To return home at eventide with gratitude;
And then to sleep with a prayer for the beloved in
    your heart and a song of praise upon your lips.

KAHLIL GIBRAN (1883–1931)

from Unending Love

I seem to have loved you in numberless forms, numberless times,
In life after life, in age after age forever.
My spell-bound heart has made and re-made the necklace of songs
That you take as a gift, wear round your neck in your many forms
In life after life, in age after age forever.

Whenever I hear old chronicles of love, its age-old pain,
Its ancient tale of being apart or together,
As I stare on and on into the past, in the end you emerge
Clad in the light of a pole-star piercing the darkness of time:
You become an image of what is remembered forever . . .

RABINDRANATH TAGORE (1861–1941)

from A Natural History of Love

Love. What a small word we use for an idea so immense and powerful it has altered the flow of history, calmed monsters, kindled works of art, cheered the forlorn, turned tough guys to mush, consoled the enslaved, driven strong women mad, glorified the humble, fueled national scandals, bankrupted robber barons, and made mincemeat of kings. How can love's spaciousness be conveyed in the narrow confines of one syllable? . . . Love is an ancient delirium, a desire older than civilization, with taproots stretching deep into dark and mysterious days . . .

The heart is a living museum. In each of its galleries, no matter how narrow or dimly lit, preserved forever like wondrous diatoms, are our moments of loving and being loved.

DIANE ACKERMAN (1948–)

True Love

But true love is a durable fire
In the wind ever burning;
Never sick, never old, never dead,
From itself never turning.

SIR WALTER RALEIGH (*c.* 1554–1618)

from Love

CRYSTALLISATION: THE BIRTH OF LOVE

Here is what happens to the soul:

1. Admiration
2. The lover says to himself: 'What joy to kiss her, to be kissed by her', and so on.
3. Hope. You study her perfections . . .
4. Love is born. To love is to enjoy seeing, touching, sensing with all the senses, and being as close as possible to the object of love who loves in return.
5. The first crystallisation begins. The lover who is sure of his mistress's love delights in attributing to her every possible excellence. In the end you exaggerate her qualities wildly, and see her as someone fallen from Heaven, still unknown, but certain to be yours.

If a lover's brain is left undisturbed for four and twenty hours, the result is the 'crystallisation' of the object of his thoughts:

A branch of a tree, plucked in winter, that has been stripped of its leaves and thrown deep down into one of the salt mines of Salzburg, is found, on its being taken out two or three months later, to be covered with brilliant crystals, and garnished, even to the very smallest twigs, which are often no bigger than a titmouse's foot, with innumerable sparkling diamonds; the original branch can no longer be seen.

What I have called crystallisation is that operation of the mind which turns whatever presents itself into a discovery of new perfections in the object of love.

STENDHAL (1783–1842)

How Passion Gives Way to Cuddles
Within Two Years

Lust has a lifespan of just two years, scientists believe. After this, the chemical that makes new lovers irresistible to each other seems to disappear from their systems.

But there is some consolation. As the passion fades away, a 'cuddle hormone' apparently kicks in, helping the couple to survive the loss of that first spark of romance.

Researchers in Italy used blood tests to establish the levels of a variety of hormones in volunteers. Some were just starting out with a new partner while others had been in an established relationship for years.

They found a nerve growth factor called neurotrophins exceeded normal levels in those enjoying the lovestruck early stages of romance.

But it was missing from the volunteers who had been settled with their partners for up to two years. The scientists, from the University of Pisa, Italy, found it had been replaced by oxytocin, which they nicknamed 'the cuddle hormone', in those who had been together for several years.

Oxytocin is a chemical known to induce labour and milk-production in pregnant and new mothers. However, it also seems to thrive in couples enjoying long, loving relationships.

The results were reported in the journal *Chemistry World*, published by the Royal Society of Chemistry. 'If lovers swear their feelings to be ever-lasting, the hormones tell a different story,' biochemist Michael Gross said in his report.

'It shows that different hormones are present in the blood when people are acutely in love. There is no evidence of the same hormones in people who have been in a stable relationship for many years.

'In fact the love molecules can disappear as early as 12 months after a relationship has started to be replaced by another chemical glue that keeps couples together. It may be the only thing that science can offer as a real-world analogy to Cupid's arrows.'

Research in the U.S. has already found that 'romantic love is primarily a reward system, which leads to various emotions rather than a specific emotion', the report added.

Scientists say that intense romantic love is different from both the sex drive and the development of attachment in the later phases of a relationship

Karen Harries-Rees, editor of *Chemistry World*, said: 'Only in recent years has the state of being in love come to be regarded as a sufficiently distinct physiological state to be investigated with biochemical methods.'

She said research into why the rational mind apparently went haywire during infatuation had closed in on four areas: genes, neurons, hormones, and pheromones.

A spokesman for the Royal Society of Chemistry said: 'Perhaps we should call this lust hormone molecule V for Valentine.'

Daily Mail, 1 February 2006

from Don Juan

In her first passion woman loves her lover,
In all the others all she loves is love.

LORD BYRON (1788–1824)

Fire

Love is friendship set on fire.

JEREMY TAYLOR (1613–67)

One Word

One word frees us of all the weight and pain of life; that word is love.

SOPHOCLES (*c.* 496–*c.* 405 BC)

Only End

We are born for love. It is the principle of existence and its only end.

BENJAMIN DISRAELI (1804–81)

Love

Any time that is not spent on love is wasted.

TORQUATO TASSO (1544–95)

from The Four Loves

To love at all is to be vulnerable. Love anything, and your heart will certainly be wrung and possibly be broken. If you want to make sure of keeping it intact, you must give your heart to no one, not even to an animal. Wrap it carefully round with hobbies and little luxuries; avoid all entanglements; lock it up safe in the casket or coffin of your selfishness. But in that casket – safe, dark, motionless, airless – it will change. It will not be broken; it will become unbreakable, impenetrable, irredeemable.

C. S. Lewis (1898–1963)

Aspiration

The reason why all men honor love is because it looks up, and not down; aspires and not despairs.

RALPH WALDO EMERSON (1803–82)

Crowning Grace

Love is the crowning grace of humanity, the holiest right of the soul, the golden link which binds us to duty and truth, the redeeming principle that chiefly reconciles the heart to life, and is prophetic of eternal good.

FRANCESCO PETRARCH (1304–74)

Love Alone

He whom love touches not walks in darkness. Love will make men dare to die for their beloved – love alone; and women as well as men.

PLATO (c. 427–c. 347 BC)

from Desiderata

Be yourself, especially do not feign affection. Neither be cynical about love; for in the face of all aridity and disenchantment it is as perennial as the grass.

MAX EHRMANN (1872–1945)

II

COMMITMENT

Intimacy

Sonnet XVII

I do not love you as if you were salt-rose, or topaz,
or the arrow of carnations the fire shoots off.
I love you as certain dark things are to be loved,
in secret, between the shadow and the soul.

I love you as the plant that never blooms
but carries in itself the light of hidden flowers;
thanks to your love a certain solid fragrance,
risen from the earth, lives darkly in my body.

I love you without knowing how, or when, or from where.
I love you straightforwardly, without complexities or pride;
so I love you because I know no other way

than this: where *I* does not exist, nor *you*,
so close that your hand on my chest is my hand,
so close that your eyes close as I fall asleep.

PABLO NERUDA (1904–73)

Variation on the Word *Sleep*

I would like to watch you sleeping.
I would like to watch you,
sleeping. I would like to sleep
with you, to enter
your sleep as its smooth dark wave
slides over my head

and walk with you through that lucent
wavering forest of bluegreen leaves
with its watery sun & three moons
towards the cave where you must descend,
towards your worst fear

I would like to give you the silver
branch, the small white flower, the one
word that will protect you
from the grief at the center
of your dream, from the grief
at the center. I would like to follow
you up the long stairway
again & become
the boat that would row you back
carefully, a flame
in two cupped hands
to where your body lies
beside me, and you enter
it as easily as breathing in

I would like to be the air
that inhabits you for a moment
only. I would like to be that unnoticed
& that necessary.

MARGARET ATWOOD (1939–)

To F. Scott Fitzgerald, 1919

I'D DO ANYTHING

Sweetheart,

Please, please don't be so depressed – We'll be married soon, and these lonesome nights will be over forever – and until we are, I am loving, loving every tiny minute of the day and night – Maybe you won't understand this, but sometimes when I miss you most, it's hardest to write – and you always know when I make myself – Just the ache of it all – and I *can't* tell you. If we were together, you'd feel how strong it is – you're so sweet when you're melancholy. I love your sad tenderness – when I've hurt you – That's one of the reasons I could never be sorry for our quarrels – and they bothered you so – Those dear, dear little fusses, when I always tried so hard to make you kiss and forget –

Scott – there's nothing in all the world I want but you – and your precious love – All the material things are nothing. I'd just hate to live a sordid, colorless existence – because you'd soon love me less – and less – and I'd do anything – anything – to keep your heart for my own – I don't want to live – I want to love first, and live incidentally – Why don't you feel that I'm waiting – I'll come to you, Lover, when you're ready – Don't ever think of the things you can't give me – you've trusted me with the dearest heart of all – and it's so damn much more than anybody else in all the world has ever had –

ZELDA FITZGERALD (1900–47)

In Paris with You

Don't talk to me of love. I've had an earful
And I get tearful when I've downed a drink or two.
I'm one of your talking wounded.
I'm a hostage. I'm maroonded.
I'm in Paris with you.

Yes I'm angry at the way I've been bamboozled
And resentful at the mess that I've been through.
I admit I'm on the rebound
And I don't care where are *we* bound.
I'm in Paris with you.

Do you mind if we do *not* go to the Louvre,
If we say sod off to sodding Notre Dame,
If we skip the Champs Elysées
And remain here in this sleazy
Old hotel room
Doing this and that
To what and whom
Learning who you are,
Learning what I am.

Don't talk to me of love. Let's talk of Paris,
The little bit of Paris in our view.
There's that crack across the ceiling
And the hotel walls are peeling
And I'm in Paris with you.

JAMES FENTON (1949–)

A Dedication to My Wife

To whom I owe the leaping delight
That quickens my senses in our wakingtime
And the rhythm that governs the repose of our sleepingtime,
   The breathing in unison.

Of lovers whose bodies smell of each other
Who think the same thoughts without need of speech,
And babble the same speech without need of meaning.

No peevish winter wind shall chill
No sullen tropic sun shall wither
The roses in the rose-garden which is ours and ours only

But this dedication is for others to read:
These are private words addressed to you in public.

T. S. ELIOT (1888–1965)

Intimacy

Since I have seen you do those intimate things
that other men but dream of; lull asleep
the sinister dark forest of your hair
and tie the bows that stir on your calm breast
faintly as leaves that shudder in their sleep;
since I have seen your stocking swallow up,
a swift black wind, the flame of your pale foot,
and deemed your slender limbs so meshed in silk
sweet mermaid sisters drowned in their dark hair;
I have not troubled overmuch with food,
and wine has seemed like water from a well;
pavements are built of fire, grass of thin flames;
all other girls grow dull as painted flowers,
or flutter harmlessly like coloured flies
whose wings are tangled in the net of leaves
spread by frail trees that grow behind the eyes.

EDGELL RICKWORD (1898–1982)

To John Middleton Murry, 1917

Last night, before you got into bed, you stood, quite naked, bending forward a little, talking. It was only for an instant. I saw you – I loved you so, loved your body with such tenderness. Ah, my dear! And I am not thinking now of 'passion'. No, of that other thing that makes me feel that every inch of you is so precious to me – your soft shoulders – your creamy warm skin, your ears cold like shells are cold – your long legs and your feet that I love to clasp with my feet – the feeling of your belly – and your thin young back. Just below that bone that sticks out at the back of your neck you have a little mole. It is partly because we are young that I feel this tenderness. I love your youth. I could not bear that it should be touched even by a cold wind if I were the Lord.

We two, you know, have everything before us, and we shall do very great things. I have perfect faith in us, and so perfect is my love for you that I am, as it were, still, silent to my very soul. I want nobody but you for my lover and my friend and to nobody but you shall I be faithful.

I am yours for ever

Tig

KATHERINE MANSFIELD (1888–1923)

Close close all night . . .

Close close all night
the lovers keep.
They turn together
in their sleep,

close as two pages
in a book
that read each other
in the dark.

Each knows all
the other knows,
learned by heart
from head to toes.

ELIZABETH BISHOP (1911–79)

To Wed or Not to Wed?

To Wed or Not to Wed

(With apologies to Shakespeare)

To wed, or not to wed: that is the question:
Whether 'tis nobler in the mind to suffer
The fret and loneliness of spinsterhood
Or to take arms against the single state
And by marrying, end it? To wed; to match,
No more; yet by this match to say we end
The heartache and the thousand natural shocks
That flesh is heir to; 'tis a consummation
Devoutly to be wish'd. To wed, to match;
To match, perchance mismatch: aye there's the rub;
For in that match what dread mishaps may come,
When we have shuffled off this single state
For wedded bliss: there's the respect
That makes singleness of so long a life,
For who'd forgo the joys of wife and mother,
The pleasures of devotion, of sacrifice and love,
The blessings of a home and all home means,
The restful sympathy of soul to soul,
The loving ones circling round at eventide
When she herself might gain all these
With a marriage vow? . . .

UNA MARSON (1905–65)

This Is the Question

Pencilled notes written in 1837 or 1838

MARRY

Children – (if it please God) – constant companion, (friend in old age) who will feel interested in one, object to be loved and played with – better than a dog anyhow – Home, and someone to take care of house – Charms of music and female chit-chat. These things good for one's health. Forced to visit and receive relations *but terrible loss of time.*

My God, it is intolerable to think of spending one's whole life, like a neuter bee, working, working and nothing after all. – No, no won't do. –

Imagine living all one's day solitarily in smoky dirty London House. – Only picture to yourself a nice soft wife on a sofa with good fire, and books and music perhaps – compare this vision with the dingy reality of Grt Marlboro' St. Marry – Marry – Marry Q.E.D.

Not MARRY

No children, (no second life) no one to care for one in old age. – What is the use of working without sympathy from near and dear friends – who are near and dear friends to the old except relatives.

Freedom to go where one liked – Choice of Society *and little of it.* Conversation of clever men at clubs. –

Not forced to visit relatives, and to bend in every trifle – to have the expense and anxiety of children – perhaps quarrelling.

Loss of time – cannot read in the evenings – fatness and idleness – anxiety and responsibility – less money for books etc. – if many children forced to gain one's bread. – (But then it is very bad for one's health to work too much.)

Perhaps my wife won't like London; then the sentence is banishment and degradation with indolent idle fool –

It being proved necessary to marry – When? Soon or Late. The Governor says soon for otherwise bad if one has children – one's character is more flexible – one's feelings more lively, and if one does not marry soon, one misses so much good pure happiness. –

But then if I married tomorrow: there would be an infinity of trouble and expense in getting and furnishing a house, – fighting about no Society – morning calls – awkwardness – loss of time every day – (without one's wife was an angel and made one keep industrious) – Then how should I manage all my business if I were obliged to go every day walking with my wife. – Eheu!! I never should know French, – or see the Continent, – or go to America, or go up in a Balloon, or take solitary trip in Wales – poor slave, you will be worse than a negro – And then horrid poverty (without one's wife was better than an angel and had money) – Never mind my boy – Cheer up – One cannot live this solitary life, with groggy old age, friendless and cold and childless staring one in one's face, already beginning to wrinkle. Never mind, trust to chance – keep a sharp look out. – There is many a happy slave –

CHARLES DARWIN (1809–82)

He married Emma Wedgwood on 29 January 1839.

from The Anatomy of Melancholy

'Tis a hazard both ways I confess, to live single or to marry, *Nam et uxorem ducere, et non ducere malum est*, it may be bad, it may be good, as it is a cross and calamity on the one side, so 'tis a sweet delight, an incomparable happiness, a blessed estate, a most unspeakable benefit, a sole content, on the other, 'tis all in the proof. Be not then so wayward, so covetous, so distrustful, so curious and nice, but let's all marry.

ROBERT BURTON (1577–1640)

Sonnet LXIX

Maybe nothingness is to be without your presence,
without you moving, slicing the noon
like a blue flower, without you walking
later through the fog and the cobbles,

without the light you carry in your hand,
golden, which maybe others will not see,
which maybe no one knew was growing
like the red beginnings of a rose.

In short, without your presence: without your coming
suddenly, incitingly, to know my life,
gust of a rosebush, wheat of wind:

since then I am because you are,
since then you are, I am, we are,
and through love I will be, you will be, we'll be.

PABLO NERUDA (1904–73)

The Confirmation

Yes, yours, my love, is the right human face.
I in my mind had waited for this long,
Seeing the false and searching for the true,
Then found you as a traveller finds a place
Of welcome suddenly amid the wrong
Valleys and rocks and twisting roads. But you,
What shall I call you? A fountain in a waste,
A well of water in a country dry,
Or anything that's honest and good, an eye
That makes the whole world bright. Your open heart,
Simple with giving, gives the primal deed,
The first good world, the blossom, the blowing seed,
The hearth, the steadfast land, the wandering sea.
Not beautiful or rare in every part.
But like yourself, as they were meant to be.

EDWIN MUIR (1887–1959)

from the film When Harry Met Sally, 1989

BILLY CRYSTAL TO MEG RYAN

I love that you get cold when it is 71 degrees out. I love that it takes you an hour and a half to order a sandwich. I love that you get a little crinkle in your nose when you're looking at me like I'm nuts. I love that after I spend the day with you, I can still smell your perfume on my clothes. And I love that you are the last person I want to talk to before I go to sleep at night. And it's not because I'm lonely, and it's not because it's New Year's Eve. I came here tonight because when you realise you want to spend the rest of your life with somebody, you want the rest of your life to start as soon as possible.

NORA EPHRON (1941–)

from Preface to Getting Married

Now things are so ill arranged that some people are born monogamous, that is, faithful, which is not a virtue but a quality, while others are born polygamous, that is, unfaithful. If these two opposites come together the result is great misery.

AUGUST STRINDBERG (1849–1912)

Pedigree

Man scans with scrupulous care the character and pedigree of his horses, cattle and dogs before he matches them: but when he comes to his own marriage he rarely, or never, takes any such care.

CHARLES DARWIN (1809–82)

A Slice of Wedding Cake

Why have such scores of lovely, gifted girls
    Married impossible men?
Simple self-sacrifice may be ruled out,
    And missionary endeavour, nine times out of ten.

Repeat 'impossible men': not merely rustic,
    Foul-tempered or depraved
(Dramatic foils chosen to show the world
    How well women behave, and always have behaved).

Impossible men: idle, illiterate,
    Self-pitying, dirty, sly,
For whose appearance even in City parks
    Excuses must be made to casual passers-by.

Has God's supply of tolerable husbands
    Fallen, in fact, so low?
Or do I always over-value woman
    At the expense of man?

            Do I?
                It might be so.

ROBERT GRAVES (1895–1985)

Old Rigmarole

He criticised her puddings and he
didn't like her cake
He wished she'd make the
biscuits that his mother used to bake
She didn't wash the dishes and
she didn't make the stew
She didn't mend his stockings
like his mother used to do
Oh, well she was not perfect,
though she tried to do her best,
Until at last she thought it was
time she had a rest
So one day when he said the
same old rigmarole all through
She turned and boxed his ears –
just as his mother used to do.

ANONYMOUS

from Marriage

Should I get married? Should I be good?
Astound the girl next door with my velvet suit and faustus hood?
Don't take her to movies but to cemeteries
tell all about werewolf bathtubs and forked clarinets
then desire her and kiss her and all the preliminaries
and she going just so far and I understanding why
not getting angry saying You must feel! It's beautiful to feel!
Instead take her in my arms lean against an old crooked tombstone
and woo her the entire night the constellations in the sky –

When she introduces me to her parents
back straightened, hair finally combed, strangled by a tie,
should I sit knees together on their 3rd degree sofa
and not ask Where's the bathroom?
How else to feel other than I am,
often thinking Flash Gordon soap –
O how terrible it must be for a young man
seated before a family and the family thinking
We never saw him before! He wants our Mary Lou!
After tea and homemade cookies they ask What do you do for a
    living?

Should I tell them: Would they like me then?
Say All right get married, we're losing a daughter
but we're gaining a son –
And should I then ask Where's the bathroom?

O God, and the wedding! All her family and her friends
and only a handful of mine all scroungy and bearded
just wait to get at the drinks and food –
And the priest! he looking at me as if I masturbated
asking me Do you take this woman for your lawful wedded wife?
And I trembling what to say say Pie Glue!
I kiss the bride all those corny men slapping me on the back
She's all yours, boy! Ha-ha-ha!

GREGORY CORSO (1930–2001)

To Anne Boleyn *c.* 1528

In debating with myself the contents of your letters I have been put to a great agony; not knowing how to understand them, whether to my disadvantage as shown in some places, or to my advantage as in others. I beseech you now with all my heart definitely to let me know your whole mind as to the love between us; for necessity compels me to plague you for a reply, having been for more than a year now struck by the dart of love, and being uncertain either of failure or of finding a place in your heart and affection, which point has certainly kept me for some time from naming you my mistress, since if you only love me with an ordinary love the name is not appropriate to you, seeing that it stands for an uncommon position very remote from the ordinary; but if it pleases you to do the duty of a true, loyal mistress and friend, and to give yourself body and heart to me, who have been, and will be, your very loyal servant (if your rigour does not forbid me), I promise you that not only the name will be due to you, but also to take you as my sole mistress, casting off all others than yourself out of mind and affection, and to serve you only; begging you to make me a complete reply to this my rude letter as to how far and in what I can trust; and if it does not please you to reply in writing, to let me know of some place where I can have it by word of mouth, the which place I will seek out with all my heart. No more for fear of wearying you. Written by the hand of him who would willingly remain your

HR

HENRY VIII (1491–1547)

The king had her beheaded in 1536.

To Diana Manners, 1918

Darling, my darling – One line in haste to tell you that I love you more today than ever in my life before, that I never see beauty without seeing you or scent happiness without thinking of you.

You have fulfilled all my ambition, realized all my hopes, made all my dreams come true. You have set a crown of roses on my youth and fortified me against the disaster of our days. Your courageous gaiety has inspired me with joy. Your tender faithfulness has been a rock of security and comfort. I have felt for you all kinds of love at once. I have asked much of you and you have never failed me. You have intensified all colours, heightened all beauty, deepened all delight. I love you more than life, my beauty, my wonder.

Duff

DUFF COOPER (1890–1954)

I'll Be There

I'll be there, my darling,
Through thick and through thin
When your mind is a mess
When your head's in a spin
When your plane's been delayed
When you've missed the last train
When life is just threatening
To drive you insane
When your thrilling whodunnit
Has lost its last page
When somebody tells you
You're looking your age
When your coffee's too cool
And your wine is too warm
When the forecast said 'Fine'
But you're out in a storm
When you ordered the korma
But got the Madras
When you wake in the night
And are sure you smell gas
When your quick-break hotel
Is more like a slum
And your holiday photos
Show only your thumb
When you park for five minutes
In a residents' bay
And return to discover
You've been towed away
When the jeans that you bought
In hope or in haste
Stick on your hips
And won't reach round your waist
When the dentist looks into
Your mouth and just sighs
When your heroes turn out

To be wimps in disguise
When the food you most like
Brings you out in red rashes
When as soon as you boot up
The bloody thing crashes
When you're in extra time
And the other team scores
When someone informs you
There's no Santa Claus
When you gaze at the stars
And step on a nail
When you know you'll succeed
But, somehow, you fail
When your horoscope tells you
You'll have a good day
So you ask for a rise
And your boss says, 'No way.'

So my darling, my sweetheart, my dear . . .
When you spill your beer
When you shed a tear
When you burn the toast
When you miss the post
When you lose the plot
When I'm all you've got
When you break a rule
When you act the fool
When you've got the flu
When you're in a stew
When you're last in the queue
Don't feel blue
'Cause I'm telling you
I'll be there
        I'll be there
                I'll be there for you.

LOUISE CUDDON (1971–)

Prayer to St Catherine

St Catherine, St Catherine, O lend me thine aid,
And grant that I never may die an old maid.

A husband, St Catherine,
A *good* one, St Catherine;
But arn–a–one better than
Narn–a–one, St Catherine.

Sweet St Catherine,
A husband, St Catherine,
Handsome, St Catherine,
Rich, St Catherine.
Soon, St Catherine!

ANONYMOUS

St Catherine is the patron saint of spinsters.

The Question

When marrying, ask yourself this question: Do you believe that you will be able to converse well with this person into your old age? Everything else in marriage is transitory.

FRIEDRICH NIETZSCHE (1844–1900)

from Jeeves in the Offing

I was in rare fettle and the heart had touched a new high. I don't know anything that braces one up like finding you haven't got to get married after all.

P. G. WODEHOUSE (1881–1975)

Beauty

Remember if you marry for beauty, thou bindest thyself all thy life for that which perchance, will neither last nor please thee one year: and when thou hast it, it will be to thee of no price at all.

EMILY DICKINSON (1830–86)

Scottish Proverb

Never marry for money. Ye'll borrow it cheaper.

ANONYMOUS

The Knock at the Door

The whole purpose of a husband and wife is that when hard times knock at the door you should be able to embrace each other.

NELSON MANDELA (1918–)

Risk

There is no greater risk, perhaps, than matrimony, but there is nothing happier than a happy marriage.

BENJAMIN DISRAELI (1804–81)

Proposals

Proposals

Say Yes

Sukey, you shall be my wife
   And I will tell you why:
I have got a little pig,
   And you have got a sty;
I have got a dun cow
   And you can make good cheese;
Sukey, will you marry me?
   Say Yes, if you please.

ANONYMOUS

Will Not That Do?

Quoth John to Joan, will thou have me:
I prithee now, wilt? and I'll marry thee,
My cow, my calf, my house, my rents,
And all my lands and tenements:
    Oh, say, my Joan, will not that do?
    I cannot come every day to woo.

I've corn and hay in the barn hard-by,
And three fat hogs pent up in the sty,
I have a mare and she is coal black,
I ride on her tail to save my back.
    Then, say, my Joan, will not that do?
    I cannot come every day to woo.

I have a cheese upon the shelf,
And I cannot eat it all myself;
I've three good marks that lie in a rag,
In a nook of the chimney, instead of a bag.
    Then, say, my Joan, will not that do?
    I cannot come every day to woo.

To marry I would have thy consent,
But faith I never could compliment;
I can say nought but 'Hoy, gee ho!'
Words that belong to the cart and the plough.
    Oh, say, my Joan, will not that do?
    I cannot come every day to woo.

ANONYMOUS

Be Married

I feel sad when I don't see you. Be married, why won't you? And come to live with me. I will make you as happy as I can. You shall not be obliged to work hard; and when you are tired; you may lie in my lap and I will sing you to rest . . . I will play you a tune upon the violin as often as you ask and as well as I can; and leave off smoking, if you say so . . . I would always be very kind to you, I think, because I love you so well. I will not make you bring in wood and water, or feed the pig, or milk the cow, or go to the neighbors to borrow milk. Will you be married?

ANONYMOUS

Cheeky Proposal to the Local Beauty in Middlemoor, Yorkshire

29 November 1866

My Dear Miss,

I now take up my pen to write to you hoping these few lines will find you well as it leaves me at present Thank God for it. You will perhaps be surprised that I should make so bold as to write to you who is such a lady and I hope you will not be vex at me for it. I hardly dare say what I want, I am so timid about ladies, and my heart trimmels like a hespin. But I once seed in a book that faint heart never won fair lady, so here goes.

I am a farmer in a small way and my age is rather more than forty years and my mother lives with me and keeps my house, and she has been very poorly lately and cannot stir about much and I think I should be more comfortabler with a wife.

I have had my eye on you a long time and I think you are a very nice young woman and one that would make me happy if only you think so. We keep a servant girl to milk three kye and do the work in the house, and she goes out a bit in the summer to gadder wickens and she snags a few of turnips in the back kend. I do a piece of work on the farm myself and attends Pately Market, and I sometimes show a few sheep and I feeds between 3 & 4 pigs agen Christmas, and the same is very useful in the house to make pies and cakes and so forth, and I sells the hams to help pay for the barley meal.

I have about 73 pund in Naisbro Bank and we have a nice little parlour downstairs with a blue carpet, and an oven on the side of the fireplace and the old woman on the other side smoking. The Golden Rules claimed up on the walls above the long settle, and you could sit all day in the easy chair and knit and mend my kytles and leggums, and you could make the tea ready agin I come in, and you could make butter for Pately Market, and I would drive you to church every Sunday in the spring cart, and I would do all that bees in my power to make you happy. So I hope to hear from you. I am in desprit and

Yurnest, and will marry you at May Day, or if my mother dies afore I shall want you afore. If only you will accept of me, my dear, we could be very happy together.

I hope you will let me know your mind by return of post, and if you are favourable I will come up to scratch. So no more at present from your well-wisher and true love –

Simon Fallowfield

P.S. I hope you will say nothing about this. If you will not accept of me I have another very nice woman in my eye, and I think I shall marry her if you do not accept of me, but I thought you would suit me mother better, she being very crusty at times. So I tell you now before you come, she will be Maister.

She refused.

Worldly Goods, 1712

Lovely (and oh, that I could write loving) Mistress Margaret Clark, I pray you let affection excuse presumption. Having been so happy as to enjoy the sight of your sweet countenance, I am so enamoured with you that I can no more keep close my flaming desire to become your servant.

And I am the more bold now to write to your sweet self because I am now my own man, and may match where I please, for my father is taken away, and now I am come to my living, which is Ten Yard Land and a House, and there is never a yard of land in our field but is well worth ten pounds a year; and all my brothers and sisters are provided for.

Besides I have good household stuff, though I say it, both of brass and pewter, linens and woollens; and, though my house be thatched, it shall go hard but I will have one half of it slated.

If you think well of this motion I will wait upon you as soon as my new clothes are made and the hay harvest is in.

Anonymous

A Subaltern's Love-Song

Miss J. Hunter Dunn, Miss J. Hunter Dunn,
Furnish'd and burnish'd by Aldershot sun,
What strenuous singles we played after tea,
We in the tournament — you against me!

Love-thirty, love-forty, oh! weakness of joy,
The speed of a swallow, the grace of a boy,
With carefullest carelessness, gaily you won,
I am weak from your loveliness, Joan Hunter Dunn.

Miss Joan Hunter Dunn, Miss Joan Hunter Dunn
How mad I am, sad I am, glad that you won.
The warm-handled racket is back in its press,
But my shock-headed victor, she loves me no less.

Her father's euonymus shines as we walk,
And swing past the summer-house, buried in talk
And cool the verandah that welcomes us in
To the six-o'clock news and a limejuice and gin.

The scent of the conifers, sound of the bath,
The view from my bedroom of moss-dappled path,
As I struggle with double-end evening tie,
For we dance at the Golf Club, my victor and I.

On the floor of her bedroom lie blazer and shorts
And the cream-coloured walls are be-trophied with sports,
And westering, questioning settles the sun
On your low-leaded window, Miss Joan Hunter Dunn.

The Hillman is waiting, the light's in the hall,
The pictures of Egypt are bright on the wall,
My sweet, I am standing beside the oak stair
And there on the landing's the light on your hair.

By roads not 'not adopted', by woodlanded ways,
She drove to the club in the late summer haze,
Into nine-o'clock Camberley, heavy with bells
And mushroomy, pine-woody, evergreen smells.

Miss Joan Hunter Dunn, Miss Joan Hunter Dunn,
I can hear from the car park the dance has begun.
Oh! full Surrey twilight! importunate band!
Oh! strongly adorable tennis-girl's hand!

Around us are Rovers and Austins afar,
Above us, the intimate roof of the car
And here on my right is the girl of my choice,
With the tilt of her nose and the chime of her voice,

And the scent of her wrap, and the words never said,
And the ominous, ominous dancing ahead.
We sat in the car park till twenty to one
And now I'm engaged to Miss Joan Hunter Dunn.

JOHN BETJEMAN (1906–84)

from a letter, 1840

LOVE TOO FREELY REVEALED

No young lady should fall in love, till the offer has been made, accepted – the marriage ceremony performed and the first year of wedded life has passed away – a woman may then begin to love, but with great precaution –very coolly – very moderately – very rationally – if she ever love so much that a harsh word or cold look from her husband cuts her to the heart – she is a fool . . .

. . . Did I not once tell you of an instance of a Relative of mine who cared for a young lady till he began to suspect that she cared more for him and then instantly conceived a sort of contempt for her? You know to what I allude – never as you value your ears mention the circumstance – but I have two studies – *you* are my study for the success, the credit, and the respectability of a quiet, tranquil character. Mary is my study – for the contempt, the remorse – the misconstruction which follow the development of feelings in themselves noble, warm – generous – devoted and profound – but which being too freely revealed – too frankly bestowed – are not estimated at their real value.

CHARLOTTE BRONTË (1816–55)

from Under Milk Wood

MAD WITH LOVE

MR EDWARDS: Myfanwy Price!

MISS PRICE: Mr Mog Edwards!

MR EDWARDS: I am a draper mad with love. I love you more than all the flannelette and calico, candlewick, dimity, crash and merino, tussore, cretonne, crepon, muslin, poplin, ticking and twill in the whole Cloth Hall of the world. I have come to take you away to my Emporium on the hill, where the change hums on wires. Throw away your little bedsocks and your Welsh wool knitted jacket, I will warm the sheets like an electric toaster, I will lie by your side like the Sunday roast.

MISS PRICE: I will knit you a wallet of forget-me-not blue, for the money to be comfy. I will warm your heart by the fire so that you can slip it in under your vest when the shop is closed.

MR EDWARDS: Myfanwy, Myfanwy, before the mice gnaw at your bottom drawer will you say

MISS PRICE: Yes, Mog, yes, Mog, yes, yes, yes.

MR EDWARDS: And all the bells of the tills of the town shall ring for our wedding.

DYLAN THOMAS (1914–53)

from The Tempest

MIRANDA: I do not know
    One of my sex; no woman's face remember,
    Save, from my glass, mine own; nor have I seen
    More that I may call men than you, good friend,
    And my dear father: how features are abroad,
    I am skilless of; but, by my modesty,
    The jewel in my dower, I would not wish
    Any companion in the world but you;
    Nor can imagination form a shape,
    Besides yourself, to like of. But I prattle
    Something too wildly, and my father's precepts
    I therein do forget.
FERDINAND: I am, in my condition,
    A prince, Miranda; I do think, a king;
    I would not so! – and would no more endure
    This wooden slavery than to suffer
    The flesh-fly blow my mouth. Hear my soul speak:
    The very instant that I saw you, did
    My heart fly to your service; there resides,
    To make me slave to it; and for your sake
    Am I this patient log-man.
MIRANDA: Do you love me?
FERDINAND: O heaven, O earth, bear witness to this sound,
    And crown what I profess with kind event
    If I speak true! if hollowly, invert
    What best is boded me to mischief! I,
    Beyond all limit of what else i' the world,
    Do love, prize, honour you.
MIRANDA: I am a fool
    To weep at what I am glad of.
PROSPERO: Fair encounter
    Of two most rare affections! Heavens rain grace

On that which breeds between 'em!

FERDINAND: Wherefore weep you?

MIRANDA: At mine unworthiness, that dare not offer
  What I desire to give; and much less take
  What I shall die to want. But this is trifling;
  And all the more it seeks to hide itself
  The bigger bulk it shows. Hence, bashful cunning!
  And prompt me, plain and holy innocence!
  I am your wife, if you will marry me;
  If not, I'll die your maid: to be your fellow
  You may deny me; but I'll be your servant,
  Whether you will or no.

FERDINAND: My mistress, dearest;
  And I thus humble ever.

MIRANDA: My husband, then?

FERDINAND: Ay, with a heart as willing
  As bondage e'er of freedom: here's my hand.

MIRANDA: And mine, with my heart in't: and now farewell
  Till half an hour hence.

FERDINAND: A thousand thousand!

WILLIAM SHAKESPEARE (1564–1616)

The Foggy Dew

When I was a batchelor early and young,
    I followed the weaving trade,
And all the harm ever I done,
    Was courting a servant maid.
I courted her the summer season,
    And part of the winter too,
And many a night I rolled her in my arms,
    All over the Foggy dew.

One night as I lay on my bed,
    As I laid fast asleep,
There came a pretty fair maid,
    And most bitterly did weep.
She wept she mourned she tore her hair,
    Crying, alas what shall I do,
This night I'm resolved to come to bed with you
    For fear of the Foggy dew.

It was in the first part of the night,
    We both did sport and play,
And in the latter part of the night.
    She slept in my arms till day.
When broad day-light did appear,
    She cried I am undone,
Hold your tongue you foolish girl,
    The Foggy dew is gone.

Suppose that we should have a child,
    It would cause us to smile,
Suppose that we should have another
    It would make us laugh awhile.
Suppose that we should have another,
    And another one too,

Would make you leave off your foolish tricks
And think no more of the Foggy dew.

I love this young girl dearly,
    I loved her as my life,
Took this girl and married her,
    And made her my lawful wife.
Never told her of her faults,
    Nor never intend to do,
But every time she winks or smiles,
    She thinks of the Foggy dew.

ANONYMOUS

from The Life of Samuel Johnson

MADE FOR EACH OTHER?

We all met at dinner at Mr Lloyd's, where we were entertained with great hospitality. Mr and Mrs Lloyd had been married the same year with their Majesties, and like them, had been blessed with a numerous family of fine children, their numbers being exactly the same. Johnson said, 'Marriage is the best state for a man in general; and every man is a worse man, in proportion as he is unfit for the married state' . . .

. . . When he again talked on Mrs Careless tonight, he seemed to have had his affection revived, for he said, 'If I had married her, it might have been as happy for me.' BOSWELL. 'Pray, Sir, do you not suppose that there are fifty women in the world, with any one of whom a man may be as happy, as with any one woman in particular?' JOHNSON. 'Ay, Sir, fifty thousand.' BOSWELL 'Then, Sir, you are not of opinion with some who imagine that certain men and certain women are made for each other; and that they cannot be happy if they miss their counterparts?' JOHNSON. 'To be sure not, Sir. I believe marriages would in general be as happy, and often more so, if they were all made by the Lord Chancellor, upon a due consideration of characters and circumstances without the parties having any choice in the matter.'

JAMES BOSWELL (1740–95)

143

A Formal Written Proposal and Acceptance, 1883

Much Esteemed Friend.

Allow me to bring our mutual agreement to canvass our marital adaptations to this distinct issue. I hereby offer you my hand, heart and whole being in marriage, on this sole condition, that you *reciprocate* with yours. I will bestow my whole souled love and affection on you, if you can and will bestow yours on me; but not otherwise. Do you accord me this privilege, on this condition? If yes, please say wherein I can improve myself in your estimation and I will do my utmost to please you.

I *wish* you had better health, rose earlier, knew more about housekeeping &c., yet these are minor matters compared with your many conjugal excellencies. Deliberate fully, and if you wish to know more of me in order to decide, ask – or –. Your answer, as soon as you can fully decide upon this life affair, will much oblige,

Yours truly, AB.

Dear Sir:

I accept your proffer of your hand and heart in marriage and on its only condition, that I return my own; which I now do by consecrating my whole existence to you alone. Since you are mine, *let me make the most of you* by obviating your faults and developing your excellencies, that I may love you the better. Abstaining from tobacco will enhance my affection for you, yet do as you please I will try to correct the faults you mention.

Thank Heaven that you are finally mine, and I yours, to love and live with and for, and be loved and lived with and for, and that my gushing affections can now rest on one so every way worthy of my complete devotion. We will arrange preliminaries when we meet, which I hope may be soon and often. Meanwhile, I am wholly yours.

CD.

Professor Fowler

Perfection!

After a little pause, I said to Lord M[elbourne], that I had made up my mind (about marrying dearest Albert). . . . 'I think it'll be well received; for I hear there is an anxiety now that it should be; and I'm very glad of it; I think it is a very good thing, and you'll be much more comfortable; for a woman cannot stand alone for long, in whatever situation she is.' . . . Then I asked, if I hadn't better tell Albert of my decision soon, in which Lord M. agreed. How? I asked, for that in general such things were done the other way, – which made Lord M. laugh.

15 October 1839

At about ½p. 12 I sent for Albert; he came to the Closet where I was alone, and after a few minutes I said to him, that I thought he must be aware why I wished [him] to come here, and that it would make me too happy if he would consent to what I wished (to marry me); we embraced each other over and over again, and he was so kind, so affectionate; Oh! to feel I was, and am, loved by such an Angel as Albert was too great delight to describe! he is perfection; perfection in every way – in beauty – in everything! I told him I was quite unworthy of him and kissed his dear hand – he said he would be very happy [to share his life with her] and was so kind and seemed so happy, that I really felt it was the happiest brightest moment in my life, which made up for all I had suffered and endured. Oh! how I adore and love him, I cannot say!! how I will strive to make him feel as little as possible the great sacrifice he has made; I told him it was a great sacrifice, – which he wouldn't allow . . . I feel the happiest of human beings.

QUEEN VICTORIA (1819–1901)

Yes, I'll Marry You, My Dear

Yes, I'll marry you, my dear, and here's the reason why:
So I can push you out of bed when the baby starts to cry,
And if we hear a knocking and it's creepy and it's late,
I hand you the torch you see and *you* investigate.

Yes, I'll marry you, my dear, you may not apprehend it,
But when the tumble-drier goes it's you that has to mend it,
You have to face the neighbour, should our labrador attack him,
And if a drunkard fondles me, it's *you* that has to whack him.

Yes, I'll marry you, my dear, you're virile and you're lean,
My house is like a pigsty, *you* can help to keep it clean,
That little sexy dinner which you served by candlelight,
As I just do chipolatas, you can cook it every night!

It's you who has to work the drill and put up curtain track,
And when I've got PMT it's you who gets the flak,
I *do* see great advantages, but none of them for you,
And so before you see the light, I do I do I do!

PAM AYRES (1947–)

Marry the Man Today

from Guys and Dolls, *first performed* 1950

At Wanamaker's and Saks and Klein's
A lesson I've been taught
You can't get alterations on a dress you haven't bought.

At any vegetable market from Borneo to Nome
You mustn't squeeze a melon 'till you get the melon home.

You've simply got to gamble.
You get no guarantee.
Now doesn't that kind of apply to you and I?

You and me.

Why not?

Why not what?

Marry the man today
Trouble though he may be
Much as he likes to play
Crazy and wild and free.
Marry the man today
Rather than sigh and sorrow
Marry the man today
And change his ways tomorrow

Marry the man today
Marry the man today
Maybe he's leaving town
Maybe he's leaving town
Don't let him get away
Don't let him get away

Hurry and track him down
Counter-attack him and

Marry the man today
Give him the girlish laughter.
Give him your hand today and
Save the fist for after.
Slowly introduce him to the better things
Respectable, conservative and clean.
Reader's Digest!
Guy Lombardo!
Rogers Peet!
Golf!
Galoshes!
Ovaltine!
But marry the man today
Handle it meek and gently.

Marry the man today and train him subsequently.
Carefully expose him to domestic life
And if he ever tries to stray from you
Have a pot-roast.
Have a headache.
Have a baby.
Have two!
Six!
Nine!
Stop!

But marry the man today
Rather than sigh and sorrow
Marry the man today.
And change his ways – change his ways – change his ways
tomorrow!

FRANK LOESSER (1910–69)

III

WEDDING DAY

Sharing Love

Love Comes Quietly

Love comes quietly,
finally, drops
about me, on me,
in the old ways.

What did I know
thinking myself
able to go
alone all the way.

ROBERT CREELY (1926–)

from A Wedding

Into the enormous sky flew
a whirlwind of blue-gray patches –
a flock of doves spiraling up
suddenly from the dovecotes.

And to see them makes you wish,
just as the wedding-feast is ending,
years of happiness for this couple,
flung onto the wind like doves.

BORIS PASTERNAK (1890–1960)

Old English Toast to the Bride

Love, be true to her; Life, be dear to her;
Health, stay close to her; Joy, draw near to her;
Fortune, find what you can do for her,
Search your treasure-house through for her,
Follow her footsteps the wide world over,
And keep her husband always her lover!

ANONYMOUS

Wedding

From time to time our love is like a sail
and when the sail begins to alternate
from tack to tack, it's like a swallowtail
and when the swallow flies it's like a coat;
and if the coat is yours, it has a tear
like a wide mouth and when the mouth begins
to draw the wind, it's like a trumpeter
and when the trumpet blows, it blows like millions . . .
and this, my love, when millions come and go
beyond the need of us, is like a trick;
and when the trick begins, it's like a toe
tip-toeing on a rope, which is like luck;
and when the luck begins, it's like a wedding,
which is like love, which is like everything.

ALICE OSWALD (1966–)

Love Not Me For Comely Grace

Love not me for comely grace,
For my pleasing eye or face,
Nor for any outward part,
No, nor for a constant heart:
For these may fail or turn to ill,
So thou and I shall sever:
Keep, therefore, a true woman's eye,
And love me still but know not why –
So hast thou the same reason still
To doat upon me ever!

ANONYMOUS

The Good Morrow

I wonder by my troth, what thou and I
    Did, till we loved? were we not weaned till then?
But sucked on country pleasures, childishly?
    Or snorted we i'the seven sleepers' den?
'Twas so; But this, all pleasures fancies be.
If ever any beauty I did see,
Which I desired, and got, 'twas but a dream of thee.

And now good morrow to our waking souls,
    Which watch not one another out of fear;
For love, all love of other sights controls,
    And makes one little room, an everywhere.
Let sea-discoverers to new worlds have gone,
Let maps to others, worlds on worlds have shown,
Let us possess our world, each hath one, and is one.

My face in thine eye, thine in mine appears,
    And true plain hearts do in the faces rest,
Where can we find two better hemispheres
    Without sharp North, without declining West?
Whatever dies, was not mixed equally;
If our two loves be one, or, thou and I
Love so alike. that none do slacken, none can die.

JOHN DONNE (1572–1631)

Epithalamion

Singing, today I married my white girl
beautiful in a barley field.
Green on thy finger a grass blade curled,
so with this ring I thee wed, I thee wed,
and send our love to the loveless world
of all the living and all the dead.

Now, no more than vulnerable human,
we, more than one, less than two,
are nearly ourselves in a barley field –
and only love is the rent that's due
though the bailiffs of time return anew
to all the living but not the dead.

Shipwrecked, the sun sinks down harbours
of a sky, unloads its liquid cargoes
of marigolds, and I and my white girl
lie still in the barley – who else wishes
to speak, what more can be said
by all the living against all the dead?

Come then all you wedding guests:
green ghost of trees, gold of barley,
you blackbird priests in the field,
you wind that shakes the pansy head
fluttering on a stalk like a butterfly;
come the living and come the dead.

Listen flowers, birds, winds, worlds,
tell all today that I married
more than a white girl in the barley –
for today I took to my human bed
flower and bird and wind and world,
and all the living and all the dead.

DANNIE ABSE (1923–)

How Do I Love Thee? Let Me Count the Ways

How do I love thee? Let me count the ways.
I love thee to the depth and breadth and height
My soul can reach, when feeling out of sight
For the ends of Being and ideal Grace.
I love thee to the level of every day's
Most quiet need, by sun and candle-light.
I love thee freely, as men strive for Right;
I love thee purely, as they turn from Praise.
I love thee with the passion put to use
In my old griefs, and with my childhood's faith:
I love thee with a love I seemed to lose
With my lost saints, – I love thee with the breath,
Smiles, tears, of all my life! – and, if God choose,
I shall but love thee better after death.

ELIZABETH BARRETT BROWNING (1806–61)

from Paradise Lost

To the Nuptial Bowre
I led her blushing like the Morn: all Heav'n,
And happie Constellations on that houre
Shed their selectest influence; the Earth
Gave sign of gratulation, and each Hill;
Joyous the Birds; fresh Gales and gentle Aires
Whisper'd it to the Woods, and from thir wings
Flung Rose, flung Odours from the spicie Shrub,
Disporting, till the amorous Bird of Night
Sung Spousal, and bid haste the Eevning Starr
On his Hill top, to light the bridal Lamp.

JOHN MILTON (1608–74)

I Carry Your Heart with Me

i carry your heart with me(i carry it in
my heart)i am never without it(anywhere
i go you go,my dear;and whatever is done
by only me is your doing,my darling)
                                    i fear
no fate(for you are my fate,my sweet)i want
no world(for beautiful you are my world,my true)
and it's you are whatever a moon has always meant
and whatever a sun will always sing is you

here is the deepest secret nobody knows
(here is the root of the root and the bud of the bud
and the sky of the sky of a tree called life;which grows
higher than soul can hope or mind can hide)
and this is the wonder that's keeping the stars apart

i carry your heart(i carry it in my heart)

E. E. CUMMINGS (1894–1962)

Song

Do not fear to put thy feet
Naked in the river sweet;
Think not leech, or newt, or toad
Will bite thy foot, when thou hast trod:
Nor let the water rising high
As thou wad'st in, make thee cry
And sob; but ever live with me
And not a wave shall trouble thee.

JOHN FLETCHER (1579–1625)

O My Luve's Like a Red, Red Rose

O my luve's like a red, red rose,
   That's newly sprung in June;
O my luve's like the melodie
   That's sweetly play'd in tune.

As fair art thou, my bonnie lass,
   So deep in luve am I,
And I will luve thee still, my Dear,
   Till a' the seas gang dry.

Till a' the seas gang dry, my Dear,
   And the rocks melt wi' the sun!
And I will luve thee still, my Dear,
   While the sands o' life shall run.

ROBERT BURNS (1759–96)

from A Wedding Sermon, 1651

Marriage is a School and Exercise of Virtue; and though Marriage hath Cares, yet the Single Life hath Desires, which are more troublesome and more dangerous, and often end in Sin; while the Cares are but Instances of Duty, and Exercises of Piety; and therefore if Single Life hath more Privacy of devotion, yet Marriage hath more Necessities and more variety of it, and is an Exercise of more Graces.

Marriage is the proper Scene of Piety and Patience, of the Duty of Parents and the Charity of Relations; here kindness is spread Abroad, and Love is united and made firm as a Centre; Marriage is the nursery of Heaven. The Virgin sends Prayers to God; but she carries but one soul to him: but the state of Marriage fills up the Number of the Elect, and hath in it the Labour of Love, and the Delicacies of Friendship, the Blessing of Society, and the Union of Hands and Hearts. It hath in it less of Beauty, but more of Safety than the Single Life; it hath more Care, but less Danger; it is more Merry, and more Sad; is fuller of Sorrows, and fuller of Joys: it lies under more Burdens, but is supported by all the Strengths of Love and Charity, and those Burdens are delightful.

JEREMY TAYLOR (1613–67)

The Owl and the Pussy-Cat

The Owl and the Pussy-Cat went to sea
   In a beautiful pea-green boat:
They took some honey, and plenty of money
   Wrapped up in a five-pound note.
The Owl looked up to the stars above,
   And sang to a small guitar,
'O lovely Pussy, O Pussy, my love,
   What a beautiful Pussy you are,
      You are,
      You are!
   What a beautiful Pussy you are!'

Pussy said to the Owl, 'You elegant fowl,
   How charmingly sweet you sing!
Oh! let us be married; too long we have tarried:
   But what shall we do for a ring?'
They sailed away, for a year and a day,
   To the land where the bong-tree grows;
And there in a wood a Piggy-wig stood,
   With a ring at the end of his nose,
      His nose,
      His nose,
   With a ring at the end of his nose.

'Dear Pig, are you willing to sell for one shilling
   Your ring?' Said the Piggy, 'I will.'
So they took it away, and were married next day
   By the Turkey who lives on the hill.
They dined on mince and slices of quince,
   Which they ate with a runcible spoon;
And hand in hand, on the edge of the sand,
   They danced by the light of the moon,
      The moon,
      The moon,
   They danced by the light of the moon.

EDWARD LEAR (1812–88)

The Wedding

We watched them marry,
punctuating the service
with our own long looks
and your finger, twitching in my belt loop.

In the garden, beneath the
surprised arches, you winked
over the rim of a gin,
I kissed my glass in reply.

That night we shared
a row in the street,
shouting promises, exchanging vows.
Windows lit up as witnesses.

A bat blessed us overhead.

OWEN SHEERS (1974–)

Reprise

Geniuses of countless nations
Have told their love for generations
Till all their memorable phrases
Are common as goldenrod or daisies.
Their girls have glimmered like the moon,
Or shimmered like a summer noon,
Stood like lily, fled like fawn,
Now the sunset, now the dawn,
Here the princess in the tower
There the sweet forbidden flower.
Darling, when I look at you
Every aged phrase is new,
And there are moments when it seems
I've married one of Shakespeare's dreams.

OGDEN NASH (1902–71)

If Thou Must Love Me, Let It Be for Nought

If thou must love me, let it be for nought
Except for love's sake only. Do not say
'I love her for her smile – her look – her way
Of speaking gently, – for a trick of thought
That falls in well with mine, and certes brought
A sense of pleasant ease on such a day' –
For these things in themselves, beloved, may
Be changed, or change for thee, – and love, so wrought,
May be unwrought so. Neither love me for
Thine own dear pity's wiping my cheeks dry, –
A creature might forget to weep, who bore
Thy comfort long, and lose thy love thereby!
Bur love me for love's sake, that evermore
Though may'st love on, through love's eternity.

ELIZABETH BARRETT BROWNING (1806–61)

Now You Will Feel No Rain

Now you will feel no rain,
for each of you will be a shelter to the other.

Now you will feel no cold,
for each of you will be warmth to the other.

Now there is no loneliness for you;
now there is no more loneliness.

Now you are two bodies,
but there is only one life before you.

Go now to your dwelling place,
to enter into your days together.

And may your days be good
and long on the earth.

APACHE SONG

They are a Tableau at the Kissing-Gate

Maids of honour, bridegroom, bride,
the best man in a grey silk suit,
a flash to catch them in the arching
stone, confettied by a sudden gust –
an apple-tree in full white spread
beyond the reach of bone and dust.

I am the driver in a passing car:
the wedding-dress a cloud of lace.
A small hand clutching at a skirt,
some nervous bridesmaid, eight
or maybe nine years old, has seen
the blossom fall, has closed her eyes –

her head falls back into the scent,
the soundless whirr and whirl of earth-
bound petals, like sycamore seeds
on a current of air, silent helicopters
bringing light – a wedding-gift
the bride will brush away, unconsciously.

This is no ordinary act, no summer fête,
another simple wedding held in June.
This is the wind shaking the apple-tree,
the bell above the kissing-gate,
the sudden fall of blossom into light
which only love and innocence can see.

We must be held accountable to love:
where they step out together arm in arm
as newly-weds, spring-cleaned, and climb
into a waiting car beneath a summer sky,
the blossom will still fall, unstoppable –
a drift of change across a changeless time.

JANE HOLLAND (1966–)

The Fair Singer

To make a final conquest of all me,
Love did compose so sweet an enemy,
In whom both beauties to my death agree,
Joining themselves in fatal harmony,
That, while she with her eyes my heart does bind,
She with her voice might captivate my mind.

I could have fled from one but singly fair;
My disentangled soul itself might save.
Breaking the curled trammels of her hair;
But how should I avoid to be her slave,
Whose subtle art invisibly can wreath
My fetters of the very air I breathe?

It had been easy fighting in some plain,
Where victory might hang in equal choice,
But all resistance against her is vain
Who has the advantage both of eyes and voice,
And all my forces needs must be undone
She having gained both the wind and sun.

ANDREW MARVELL (1621–78)

Sonnet 29

When, in disgrace with fortune and men's eyes,
I all alone beweep my outcast state,
And trouble deaf heaven with my bootless cries,
And look upon myself, and curse my fate,
Wishing me like to one more rich in hope,
Featured like him, like him with friends possessed,
Desiring this man's art and that man's scope,
With what I most enjoy contented least;
Yet in these thoughts myself almost despising,
Haply I think on thee, and then my state,
Like to the lark at break of day arising
From sullen earth, sings hymns at heaven's gate;
    For thy sweet love remembered such wealth brings
    That then I scorn to change my state with kings.

WILLIAM SHAKESPEARE (1564–1616)

The Wedding Vow

I did not stand at the altar, I stood
at the foot of the chancel steps with my beloved,
and the minister stood on the top step
holding the open Bible. The church
was wood, painted white inside, no people – God's
stable perfectly cleaned. It was night,
Spring, outside a moat of mud,
and inside, from the rafters, flies
fell onto the open Bible and the minister
tilted it and brushed them off. We stood
beside each other, crying slightly
with fear and awe. In truth, we had married
that first night, in bed, we had been
married by our bodies, but now we stood
in history – what our bodies had said
mouth to mouth, we now said publicly,
gathered together, death. We stood
holding each other by the hand, yet I also
stood as if alone, as if alone,
just before the vow, though taken
years before, took. It was a vow
of the present and the future and yet I felt it
to have some touch on the distant past
or the distant past on it, I felt
the silent crying ghost of my
parents' marriage, there somewhere
in the bright space – perhaps one of the
plummeting flies, bouncing slightly
as it hit forsaking all others, then brushed
away. I felt as if I come
to claim a promise – the sweetness I'd inferred
from their sourness; and I felt as if
I had come congenitally unworthy to beg.
And yet, I had been working toward this love

all my life. And then it was time
to speak – he was offering me, no matter
what, his life. That is all I had to
do, there, to accept that gift
I had longed for – to say I had accepted it,
as if being asked if I breathe. Do I take?
I do. I take as he takes – we have been
practicing this. Do you bear this pleasure? I do.

SHARON OLDS (1942–)

from The Imitation of Christ

ON LOVE

Love is a mighty power,
a great and complete good.
Love alone lightens every burden, and makes rough places smooth.
It bears every hardship as though it were nothing, and renders all
bitterness sweet and acceptable.

Nothing is sweeter than love,
Nothing stronger,
Nothing higher,
Nothing wider,
Nothing more pleasant,
Nothing fuller or better in heaven or earth; for love is born of
God.

Love flies, runs and leaps for joy.
It is free and unrestrained.
Love knows no limits, but ardently transcends all bounds.
Love feels no burden, takes no account of toil,
attempts things beyond its strength.

Love sees nothing as impossible,
for it feels able to achieve all things.
It is strange and effective,
while those who lack love faint and fail.

Love is not fickle and sentimental,
nor is it intent on vanities.
Like a living flame and a burning torch,
it surges upward and surely surmounts every obstacle.

THOMAS À KEMPIS (1380–1471)

Chinese Marriage Vow

Han Dynasty, 206 BC–AD 221

O, celestial beings
Let our feelings for each other
Continue without diminishing
Only when mountains are leveled
To basins, when ocean waters run
Dry, when winter is ripped
With thunders, when the summer sky
Rains snow, and heaven and earth
Are smashed together, shall we
Ever dare to be parted.

ANONYMOUS

To My Dear and Loving Husband

If ever two were one, then surely we.
If ever man were lov'd by wife, then thee;
If ever wife was happy in a man,
Compare with me ye women if you can.
I prize thy love more than whole Mines of gold,
Or all the riches that the East doth hold.

My love is such that Rivers cannot quench,
Nor ought but love from thee, give recompence.
Thy love is such I can no way repay,
The heavens reward thee manifold I pray.
Then while we live, in love lets so persever,
That when we live no more, we may live ever.

ANN BRADSTREET (1612–72)

from Burghley's Precepts

First, when it shall please God to bring you to Man's estate, making you capable of that calling, use great providence and circumspection in the choice of your wives, as the root from whence may spring most of your future good or evil.

For it is in the choice of Wife, as in a project of Warre, wherein to erre but once is to be undone for ever . . . be informed truly of their inclination, which that there may bee a more equal sympathy, compare it with your own, how they agree; for you must know, that every good woman makes not every man a good wife, no otherwise then some one good Dish digestith with every stomack. After that, enquire diligently of her stocke and race, from whence shee sprung, and how her parents have been affected in their youth.

And as it is the safest walking ever between two extremes, so choose not a wife of such absolute perfection and Beauty, that every carnall eye shall bespeake you injury: neither so base and deformed, that breed contempt in others, and bring you to a loathed bed. Make not choice of a Dwarfe or a Foole, for from the one you may beget a race of Pigmeyes, as the other will be your daily griefe and vexation: for it will irke you so oft as you shall heare her talke and you shall continually finde to your sorrow. . . . that There is nothing so fulsome as a she-foole.

Banish drunkennesse out of your House, and affect him not that is affected thereunto: for it is a vice that impaires health, consumes wealth, and transformes a man into a beast.

Suffer not your Sonnes to passe the Alpes: for they shall exchange for their forraine travell (unless they go better fortified) but others vices for their own vertues, Pride, Blasphemy and Atheisme, for Humilitie, Reverence and Religion.

WILLIAM CECIL, LORD BURGHLEY (1520–98)

Destiny

Somewhere there waiteth in this world of ours
For one lone soul another lonely soul,
Each choosing each through all the weary hours
And meeting strangely at one sudden goal.
Then blend they, like green leaves with golden flowers,
Into one beautiful and perfect whole;
And life's long night is ended, and the way
Lies open onward to eternal day.

EDWIN ARNOLD (1832–1904)

Through a Glass Darkly

1 CORINTHIANS 13

Though I speak with the tongues of men and of angels, and have not love, I am become as sounding brass, or a tinkling cymbal. And though I have the gift of prophecy, and understand all mysteries, and all knowledge; and though I have all faith, so that I could remove mountains, and I have not love, I am nothing.

And though I bestow all my goods to feed the poor, and though I give my body to be burned, and have not love, it profiteth me nothing. Love suffereth, and is kind; love envieth not; love vaunteth not itself, is not puffed up, doth not behave itself unseemly, seeketh not her own, is not easily provoked, thinketh no evil, rejoiceth not in iniquity, but rejoiceth in truth; beareth all things, believeth all things, hopeth all things, endureth all things.

Love never faileth, but whether there be prophecies, they shall fail; whether there be tongues, they shall cease; whether there be knowledge, it shall vanish away. For we know in part, and we prophesy in part. But when that which is perfect is come, then that which is in part shall be done away.

When I was a child, I spake as a child, I understood as a child, I thought as a child: but when I became a man, I put away childish things. For now we see through a glass darkly; but then face to face. Now I know in part; but then shall I know even as also I am known. And now abideth faith, hope, love, these three; but the greatest of these is love.

Is it For Now or For Always

Is it for now or for always,
The world hangs on a stalk?
Is it a trick or a trysting place,
The woods we have found to walk?

Is it a mirage or a miracle,
Your lips that lift at mine:
And the suns like a juggler's juggling-balls,
Are they a sham or a sign?

Shine out, my sudden angel,
Break fear with breast and brow,
I take you now and for always,
For always is always now.

PHILIP LARKIN (1922–85)

Chumps Make the Best Husbands

He is a chump, you know. That's what I love about him. That and the way his ears wiggle when he gets excited. Chumps always make the best husbands. When you marry, Sally, grab a chump. Tap his forehead first, and if it rings solid, don't hesitate. All the unhappy marriages come from the husband having brains. What good are brains to a man? They only unsettle him.

P. G. WODEHOUSE (1881–1975)

from The Franklin's Tale

LOVE WILL NOT BE CONSTRAINED

Lovers must both be ready to give way
If they want long to keep company.
Love will not be constrained by mastery.
When mastery comes the god of love anon
Beats his wings, and farewell, he is gone!
Love is a thing as any spirit free.
Women by nature desire liberty,
And not to be constrained like a thrall,
And the same is true of men, if I can speak for all.
Whoever is most patient under love
Has the advantage over the other.
Patience is a high virtue, certainly,
For it achieves, as the learned have said,
That which firmness can never win.
Men should not chide or complain with each word.
Learn to put up with things, or else, I can tell you,
You'll learn to anyway, whether you want to or not.

GEOFFREY CHAUCER (1343–1400)

In My Life

Recorded by The Beatles, 1965

There are places I'll remember
All my life, though some have changed,
Some forever, not for better,
Some have gone and some remain.

All these places had their moments,
With lovers and friends I still can recall,
Some are dead and some are living,
In my life I've loved them all.

But of all these friends and lovers,
There is no one compares with you,
And these memories lose their meaning
When I think of love as something new.

Though I know I'll never lose affection
For people and things that went before,
I know I'll often stop and think about them,
In my life I'll love you more.

Though I know I'll never lose affection
For people and things that went before,
I know I'll often stop and think about them,
In my life I'll love you more.
In my life I'll love you more.

JOHN LENNON (1940–80) and
PAUL MCCARTNEY (1942–)

A Birthday

My heart is like a singing bird
    Whose nest is in a watered shoot:
My heart is like an apple-tree
    Whose boughs are bent with thickset fruit;
My heart is like a rainbow shell
    That paddles in a halcyon sea;
My heart is gladder than all these
    Because my love is come to me.

Raise me a dais of silk and down;
    Hang it with vair and purple dyes;
Carve it in doves and pomegranates,
    And peacocks with a hundred eyes;
Work it in gold and silver grapes,
    In leaves and silver fleur-de-lys;
Because the birthday of my life
    Is come, my love is come to me.

CHRISTINA ROSSETTI (1830–94)

Six Rules for a Perfect Marriage, 1883

1. Be the Perfect Man or Woman
2. Be the Perfect Gentleman or Lady
3. Share Purses and ALL Interests Together
4. Improve and Be Improved by Each Other
5. Promote Each Other's Happiness
6. Redouble Love by Redeclaring it

PROFESSOR FOWLER

He Wishes for the Cloths of Heaven

Had I the heavens' embroidered cloths,
Enwrought with golden and silver light,
The blue and the dim and the dark cloths
Of night and light and the half-light,
I would spread the cloths under your feet:
But I, being poor, have only my dreams;
I have spread my dreams under your feet;
Tread softly because you tread on my dreams.

W. B. YEATS (1865–1939)

from The Song of Solomon

My beloved speaks and says to me:
  'Arise, my love, my fair one,
    and come away;
   for now the winter is past,
   the rain is over and gone.
The flowers appear on the earth;
  the time of singing has come,
and the voice of the turtle dove
    is heard in our land.
  The fig tree puts forth its figs,
 and the vines are in blossom;
  they give forth fragrance.
 Arise my love, my fair one,
    and come away.'

Set me as a seal upon your heart,
   as a seal upon your arm;
  for love is strong as death,
  passion fierce as the grave:
  its flashes are flashes of fire,
    a raging flame.
Many waters cannot quench love,
  neither can floods drown it.
   If one offered for love
 all the wealth's of one's house,
  it would be utterly scorned.

Wedding Song

I cannot swear with any certainty
That I will always feel as I do now,
Loving you with the same fierce ecstasy,
Needing the same your lips upon my brow.
Nor can I promise stars forever bright,
Or vow green leaves will never turn to gold.
I cannot see beyond this present night
To say what promises the dawn may hold.
And yet, I know my heart must follow you
High up to hilltops, low through vales of tears,
Through golden days and days of somber hue.
And love will only deepen with the years,
Becoming sun and shadow, wind and rain,
Wine that grows mellow, bread that will sustain.

NAOMI LONG MADGETT (1923–)

from The Passionate Shepherd to His Love

Come live with me and be my love,
And we will all the pleasures prove
That valleys, groves, hills, and fields,
Woods or steepy mountain yields.

CHRISTOPHER MARLOWE (1564–93)

Similar

All weddings are similar, but every marriage is different.

JOHN BERGER (1926–)

Friendship

The most successful marriages, gay or straight, even if they begin in romantic love, often become friendships. It's the ones that become the friendships that last.

ANDREW SULLIVAN (1963–)

Infinitely More Interesting

Like everything which is not the involuntary result of fleeting emotion but the creation of time and will, any marriage, happy or unhappy, is infinitely more interesting than any romance, however passionate.

W. H. AUDEN (1907–73)

from Dr Zhivago

Love is not weakness. It is strong. Only the sacrament of marriage can contain it.

BORIS PASTERNAK (1890–1960)

from Henry V

ACT V, SCENE II

God, the best maker of all marriages,
Combine your hearts in one, your realms in one.

WILLIAM SHAKESPEARE (1564–1616)

Sharing a Life

from Captain Corelli's Mandolin

ROOTS UNDERGROUND

Love is a temporary madness, it erupts like volcanoes and then subsides. And when it subsides you have to make a decision. You have to work out whether your roots have so entwined together that it is inconceivable that you should ever part. Because this is what love is. Love is not breathlessness, it is not excitement, it is not the promulgation of promises of eternal passion, it is not the desire to mate every second minute of the day, it is not lying awake at night imagining that he is kissing every cranny of your body. No, don't blush, I am telling you some truths. That is just being 'in love', which any fool can do. Love itself is what is left over when being in love has burned away, and this is both an art and a fortunate accident. Your mother and I had it, we had roots that grew towards each other underground, and when all the pretty blossom had fallen from our branches we found that we were one tree and not two.

LOUIS DE BERNIÈRES (1954–)

The Arduous Drama

Romantic love is eternally alive; as the self's most urgent quest, as grail of our hopes of happiness, as the untarnished source of the tragic, the exalted, the extreme and the beautiful in modern life. The late twentieth century is the first to open itself up to the promise of love as the focus of universal aspirations . . .

In the marriage ceremony, that moment when falling in love is replaced by the arduous drama of staying in love, the words 'in sickness and in health, for richer, for poorer, till death do us part' set love in the temporal context in which it achieves its meaning. As time begins to elapse, one begins to love the other because they have shared the same experience . . . Selves may not intertwine; but lives do, and shared memory becomes as much a bond as the bond of the flesh . . .

Family love is this dynastic awareness of time, this shared belonging to a chain of generations . . . we collaborate together to root each other in a dimension of time longer than our own lives.

MICHAEL IGNATIEFF (1947–)

Atlas

There is a kind of love called maintenance,
Which stores the WD40 and knows when to use it;

Which checks the insurance, and doesn't forget
The milkman; which remembers to plant bulbs;

Which answers letters; which knows the way
The money goes; which deals with dentists

And Road Fund Tax and meeting trains,
And postcards to the lonely; which upholds

The permanently rickety elaborate
Structures of living; which is Atlas.

And maintenance is the sensible side of love,
Which knows what time and weather are doing
To my brickwork; insulates my faulty wiring;
Laughs at my dryrotten jokes; remembers
My need for gloss and grouting; which keeps
My suspect edifice upright in air,
As Atlas did the sky.

U. A. FANTHORPE (1929–)

Accidents of Birth

Spared by a car – or airplane – crash or
cured of malignancy, people look
around with new eyes at a newly
praiseworthy world, blinking eyes like these.

For I've been brought back again from the
fine silt, the mud where our atoms lie
down for long naps. And I've also been
pardoned miraculously for years
by the lava of chance which runs down
the world's gullies, silting us back.
Here I am, brought back, set up, not yet
happened away.

                      But it's not this random
life only, throwing its sensual
astonishments upside down on
the bloody membranes behind my eyeballs,
not just me being here again, old
needer, looking for someone to need,
but you, up from the clay yourself,
as luck would have it, and inching
over the same little eon, to
meet in a room, alive in our skins,
and the whole galaxy gaping there
and the centuries whining like gnats –
you, to teach me to see it, to see
it with you, and to offer somebody
uncomprehending, impudent thanks.

WILLIAM MEREDITH (1919–)

Even Like Two Little Bank-Dividing Brooks

Even like two little bank-dividing brooks,
    That wash the pebbles with their wanton streams,
And having ranged and searched a thousand nooks,
    Meet both at length in silver-breasted Thames
        Where in a greater current they conjoin:
So I my Best-Beloved's am, so he is mine.

Even so we met; and after long pursuit
    Even so we joined; we both became entire;
No need for either to renew a suit,
    For I was flax and he was flames of fire:
        Our firm united souls did more than twine,
So I my Best-Beloved's am, so he is mine.

If all those glittering monarchs that command
    The servile quarters of this earthly ball
Should tender in exchange their shares of land,
    I would not change my fortunes for them all:
        Their wealth is but a counter to my coin;
The world's but theirs, but my Beloved's mine.

Nay, more: if the fair Thespian ladies all
    Should heap together their diviner treasure,
That treasure should be deemed a price too small
    To buy a minute's lease of half my pleasure.
        'Tis not the sacred wealth of all the Nine
Can buy my heart from him, or his from being mine.

Nor time, nor place, nor chance, nor death can bow
    My least desires unto the least remove;
He's firmly mine by oath, I his by vow;
    He's mine by faith, and I am his by love;
        He's mine by water, I am his by wine;
Thus I my Best-Beloved's am, thus he is mine.

He is my altar, I his holy place;
    I am his guest, and he my living food;
I'm his by penitence, he mine by grace;
    I'm his by purchase, he is mine by blood;
        He's my supporting elm, and I his vine:
Thus I my Best-Beloved's am, thus he is mine.

He gives me wealth, I give him all my vows;
    I give him songs, he gives me length of days;
With wreaths of grace he crowns my conquering brows;
    And I his temples with a crown of praise,
        Which he accepts as an everlasting sign,
That I my Best-Beloved's am: that he is mine.

FRANCIS QUARLES (1592–1644)

For a Wedding

Cousin, I think the shape of a marriage
is like the shelves my parents have carried
through Scotland to London, three houses;

is not distinguished, fine, French-polished,
but plywood and tatty, made
in the first place for children to batter,

still carrying markings in green felt-tip,
but always, where there are books
and a landing, managing to fit;

that marriage has lumps like
their button-backed sofa, constantly,
shortly, about to be stuffed;

and that love grows fat
as their squinting cat, swelling
round as a loaf from her basket

I wish you years that shape, that form,
and a pond in a Sunday, urban garden;
where you'll see your joined reflection tremble,

stand and watch the waterboatmen
skate with ease across the surface tension.

KATE CLANCHY (1965–)

A Marriage

You are holding up a ceiling
with both arms. It is very heavy,
but you must hold it up, or else
it will fall down on you. Your arms
are tired, terribly tired,
and, as the day goes on, it feels
as if either your arms or the ceiling
will soon collapse.

But then,
unexpectedly,
something wonderful happens:
Someone,
a man or a woman,
walks into the room
and holds their arms up
to the ceiling beside you.

So you finally get
to take down your arms.
You feel the relief of respite,
the blood flowing back
to your fingers and arms.
And when your partner's arms tire,
you hold up your own
to relieve him again.

And it can go on like this
for many years
without the house falling.

MICHAEL BLUMENTHAL (1949–)

from Anna Karenina

Having embarked on married life, he saw at every turn that it was not at all what he had imagined. At every step he felt like a man who, after admiring the smooth, happy motion of a boat on a lake, finds himself sitting in it. It was not enough to sit quietly without rocking the boat, he had to be vigilant and never lose sight of the course he was taking, or forget that there was water beneath and all around. He must row, much as it hurt his unaccustomed hands. It was pleasant enough to look at the boat from the shore, but very hard, though very delightful, to sail it.

LEO TOLSTOY (1828–1910)

Guardians of Each Other's Solitude

Marriage is in many ways a simplification of life, and it naturally combines the strengths and wills of two young people so that, together, they seem to reach farther into the future than they did before. Above all, marriage is a new task and a new seriousness – a new demand on the strength and generosity of each partner, and a great new danger for both.

The point of marriage is not to create a quick commonality by tearing down all boundaries; on the contrary, a good marriage is one in which each partner appoints the other to be the guardian of his solitude, and thus they show each other the greatest possible trust. A merging of two people is an impossibility, and where it seems to exist, it is a hemming-in, a mutual consent that robs one party or both parties of their fullest freedom and development. But once the realization is accepted that even between the closest people infinite distances exist, a marvelous living side by side can grow up for them, if they succeed in loving the expanse between them, which gives them the possibility of always seeing each other as a whole and before an immense sky.

That is why this too must be the criterion for rejection or choice: whether you are willing to stand guard over someone else's solitude, and whether you are able to set this same person at the gate of your own depths, which he learns of only through what steps forth, in holiday clothing, out of the great darkness.

Life is self-transformation, and human relationships, which are an extract of life, are the most changeable of all, they rise and fall from minute to minute, and lovers are those for whom no moment is like any another. People between whom nothing habitual ever takes place, nothing that has already existed, but just what is new, unexpected, unprecedented. There are such connections, which must be a very great, an almost unbearable happiness, but they can occur only between very rich beings, between those who have become, each for his own sake, rich, calm, and concentrated; only if two worlds are wide and deep and individual can they be combined . . .

For the more we are, the richer everything we experience is. And those who want to have a deep love in their lives must collect and save for it, and gather honey.

RAINER MARIA RILKE (1876–1926)

from Marriage and Morals

It is . . . possible for a civilized man and woman to be happy in marriage, although if this is to be the case a number of conditions must be fulfilled. There must be a feeling of complete equality on both sides; there must be no interference with mutual freedom; there must be the most complete physical and mental intimacy; and there must be a certain similarity in regard to standards of values. (It is fatal, for example, if one values only money while the other values only good work.) Given all these conditions, I believe marriage to be the best and most important relation that can exist between two human beings. If it has not often been realized hitherto, that is chiefly because husband and wife have regarded themselves as each other's policeman. If marriage is to achieve its possibilities, husbands and wives must learn to understand that whatever the law may say, in their private lives they must be free.

BERTRAND RUSSELL (1872–1970)

Walking in One's Garden

'What do you think is probably the happiest moment in one's whole life? . . . I think it's the moment when one is walking in one's garden, perhaps picking off a few dead flowers, and suddenly one thinks: My husband lives in that house – And he loves me.'

Virginia Woolf (1882–1941)

The 5:32

She said, If tomorrow my world were torn in two,
Blacked out, dissolved, I think I would remember
(As if transfixed in unsurrendering amber)
This hour best of all the hours I knew:
When cars came backing into the shabby station,
Children scuffing the seats, and the women driving
With ribbons around their hair, and the trains arriving,
And the men getting off with tired but practised motion.

Yes, I would remember my life like this, she said:
Autumn, the platform red with Virginia creeper,
And a man coming toward me, smiling, the evening paper
Under his arm, and his hat pushed back on his head;
And wood smoke lying like haze on the quiet town,
And dinner waiting, and the sun not yet gone down.

PHYLLIS McGINLEY (1905–78)

from The Odyssey

ODYSSEUS TO NAUSICAA

May Heaven grant you in all things your heart's desire – husband, house and a happy peaceful home. For there is nothing better in this world than that a man and woman, sharing the same ideas, keep house together. It discomforts their enemies and makes the hearts of their friends glad – but they themselves know more about it than anyone.

HOMER (c. 725 BC)

The Weavers

Keenness of heart and brain,
Deftness of hand and lip –
All these are not enough
To weave a perfect stuff
Out of the difficult skein
Of this relationship.

A passionate patience we
Must also bring to bear:
Be tireless to smooth out
Coil, caffle, or knot
Before time's shuttles weave it
Into the stuff, and leave it,
A lasting blemish, there.

Thus only can we keep
Ice-clear, rock-fast, sea-deep,
Our love's integrity;
Thus only can we make
A fine and flawless cloak
To wrap us round, and cover
From wind and rain our linked lives for ever.

JAN STRUTHER (1901–53)

Husband to Wife: Party Going

Turn where the stairs bend
In this other house; statued in other light,
Allow the host to ease you from your coat.
Stand where the stairs bend,
A formal distance from me, then descend
With delicacy conscious but not false
And take my arm, as if I were someone else.

Tonight, in a strange room
We will be strangers: let our eyes be blind
To all our customary stances –
Remark how well I'm groomed,
I will explore your subtly voiced nuances
Where delicacy is conscious but not false,
And take your hand, as if you were someone else.

Home forgotten, rediscover
Among chirruping of voices, chink of glass,
Those simple needs that turned us into lovers,
How solitary was the wilderness
Until we met, took leave of hosts and guests,
And with delicate consciousness of what was false
Walked off together, as if there were no one else.

BRIAN JONES

Love in a Life

I

Room after room,
I hunt the house through
We inhabit together.
Heart, fear nothing, for, heart, thou shalt find her,
Next time, herself! – not the trouble behind her
Left in the curtain, the couch's perfume!
As she brushed it, the cornice-wreath blossomed anew:
Yon looking-glass gleamed at the wave of her feather.

II

Yet the day wears,
And door succeeds door;
I try the fresh fortune –
Range the wide house from the wing to the centre.
Still the same chance! she goes out as I enter.
Spend my whole day in the quest – who cares?
But 'tis twilight, you see, – with such suites to explore,
Such closets to search, such alcoves to importune!

ROBERT BROWNING (1812–89)

from the film Shall We Dance, 2004

We need a witness to our lives. There's a billion people on the planet . . . I mean, what does any one life really mean? But in a marriage, you're promising to care about everything. The good things, the bad things, the terrible things, the mundane things . . . all of it, all of the time, every day. You're saying, 'Your life will not go unnoticed because I will notice it. Your life will not go unwitnessed because I will be your witness.'

AUDREY WELLS (1961–)

from The Prophet

STAND TOGETHER YET NOT TOO NEAR

Then Almitra spoke again and said, And what of Marriage, master?
And he answered saying:
Together you shall be for evermore.
But let there be spaces in your togetherness.
And let the winds of the heavens dance between you.

Love one another. but make not a bond of love.
Let it rather be a moving sea between the shores of your souls.
Fill each other's cup but drink not from one cup.
Give one another of your bread but eat not from the same loaf.
Sing and dance together and be joyous, but let each one of you be
    alone,
Even as the strings of a lute are alone though they quiver with the
    same music.

Give your hearts, but not into each other's keeping.
For only the hand of life can contain your hearts.
And stand together yet not too near together:
For the pillars of the temple stand apart,
And the oak tree and the cypress grow not in each other's shadow.

KAHLIL GIBRAN (1883–1931)

from These Twain

Now and then she was so bewildered by discoveries that she came to wonder why she had married him, and why people do marry – really! The fact was that she had married him for the look in his eyes. It was a sad look, and beyond that it could not be described. Also, a little, she had married him for his bright untidy hair, and for that short oblique shake of the head which, with him, meant a greeting or an affirmative.

ARNOLD BENNETT (1867–1931)

from I Do, I Will, I Have

I know that marriage is a legal and religious alliance entered into by a man who can't sleep with the window shut and a woman who can't sleep with the window open . . .

I am quite sure that marriage is the alliance of two people one of whom never remembers birthdays and the other never forgetsam . . .

OGDEN NASH (1902–71)

Falling in Love Many Times

A successful marriage requires falling in love many times, always with the same person.

MIGNON MCLAUGHLIN (1913–83)

In and Out of Love

One advantage of marriage, it seems to me, is that when you fall out of love with each other, it keeps you together until maybe you fall in again.

JUDITH VORST

Change

Women marry men hoping they will change. Men marry women hoping they will not. So each is inevitably disappointed.

ALBERT EINSTEIN (1879–1955)

Agree on the Scenario

Every marriage [is] a narrative construct – or two narrative constructs. In unhappy marriages, I see two versions of reality rather than two people in conflict. I see a struggle for imaginative dominance going on. Happy marriages seem to me those in which the two partners agree on the scenario they are enacting.

PHYLLIS ROSE

Tiny Threads

Chains do not hold a marriage together. It is threads, hundreds of tiny threads which sew people together through the years.

SIMONE SIGNORET (1921–85)

IV

EVER AFTER

An Interesting Enterprise

from The Subversive Family

Marriage still seems to be the most *interesting* enterprise which most of us come across. With all its tediums and horrors, it has both more variety and more continuity than any other commitment we can make. Its time-scale is far grander; there are still marriages alive which are older than the Bolshevik Revolution. Its passions, both of love and hatred, are more intense. Its outcomes – children, grandchildren, heirlooms of flesh and blood – stretch away over the horizon; they are the only identifiable achievements which most of us are likely to leave behind us, even if, like many achievements, they are liable to be flawed and only partially within our control. Marriage and the family make other experiences, both pleasant and unpleasant, seem a little tame and bloodless. And it is difficult to resist the conclusion that a way of living which is both so intense and so enduring must somehow come naturally to us, that it is part of being human.

FERDINAND MOUNT (1939–)

from The Young Visiters

Ethel and Bernard returned from their Honymoon with a son and heir a nice fat baby called Ignatius Bernard. They soon had six more children four boys and three girls and some of them were twins which was very exciting.

DAISY ASHFORD (1881–1972)

Chance

Maybe you'll marry, maybe you won't. Maybe you'll have children, maybe you won't. Maybe you'll divorce at forty, maybe you'll dance the funky chicken on your seventy-fifth wedding anniversary. Whatever you do, don't congratulate yourself too much, or berate yourself either. Your choices are half chance. So are everybody else's.

KURT VONNEGUT (1922–)

from The World as Will and Idea

NATURE'S SOLE INTENTION

Whenever two people fall in love, however objective and touched even by the sublime their admiration may seem, nature's sole intention is the procreation of an individual of specific qualities. This is confirmed first and foremost by the fact that the essential element is not, as we might expect, reciprocal love, but possession, that is, physical enjoyment. To be confident of the first cannot console us at all for our being deprived of the second; on the contrary, in such a situation many a one has shot himself. On the other hand, people who are deeply in love content themselves, when they cannot gain love in return, with possession, that is, with physical enjoyment. All forced marriages offer evidence of this, as does the buying of a woman's favour, in spite of her aversion, by means of generous gifts or other offerings; and so, even, do instances of rape.

The true purpose behind the whole love-story – although the parties concerned do not know it – is the production of this particular child; how this purpose is attained is a secondary consideration . . .

From the moment when their eyes first meet with longing, this new life is kindled, and it announces itself as a future individuality, harmoniously and well integrated. They feel the longing for an actual union and fusion into a single being, in order to live henceforth only as this; and this longing is fulfilled in the child they engender. In this child the qualities passed on by both parents are fused and united in one being, and so they will live on.

ARTHUR SCHOPENHAUER (1788–1860)

A Birthday Poem for Madeleine

It was at first merely the inconvenience
– Children, we thought, would interrupt our love,
Our lovemaking, thwart our careers,
Interfere with plans for foreign travel,
Leave us less money for drink and cigarettes,
And generally be a bloody nuisance.

Then, almost without our noticing it,
There the three enchanters were, and we
Were more in love than ever, and we told
Childless friends to follow our example.

But now – three tall daughters growing taller
Every day – who am I to boast I bear
Such tall and triple responsibilities?
I should be frightened, I should run away
To sea, or to some childless woman's arms,
Or to writing poems in a lonely room.

Then I see your smile upon the pillow,
And, forgetting inconvenience, responsibility,
I answer as I can to your sweet asking,
And only hope these girls deserve their mother.

T. HARRI JONES (1921–65)

Stepmother

My stepmother
   is really nice.
She ought to wear
   a label.
I don't come in
   with a latch key, now —
my tea is on
   the table.
She doesn't nag at me
   or shout.
I often hear her
   singing.
I'm glad my dad
   had wedding bells
and I hope
   they go on ringing.

Stepmothers
   in fairy tales
are hard and cold
   as iron.
There isn't a lie
   they wouldn't tell,
or a trick
   they wouldn't try on.
But MY stepmother's
   warm and true;
she's kind and cool,
   and clever —
Yes! I've a *wicked*
   stepmother —
and I hope she stays
   for ever!

JEAN KENWARD

Complicated Liaisons

The extended family, one of the by-products of the decline of conventional marriage, is a great gain. Family parties are much more exciting now than they used to be, for they usually include a miscellaneous array of cousins legal and illegal, legitimate and illegitimate, and stepchildren and step-siblings from complicated liaisons the precise origins of which have been long forgotten. I didn't foresee any of this when I started to write in 1960. Like the family, marriage isn't what it was. It's much less constraining, much less deadly, much more inventive. The summer bird-cage has an open door, and the birds fly in and out as they will.

MARGARET DRABBLE (1939–)

from Gift from the Sea

When you love someone, you do not love them all the time, in exactly the same way, from moment to moment. It is an impossibility. It is even a lie to pretend to. And yet this is exactly what most of us demand. We have so little faith in the ebb and flow of life, of love, of relationships. We leap at the flow of the tide and resist in terror its ebb. We are afraid it will never return. We insist on permanency, on duration, on continuity; when the only continuity possible, in life as in love, is in growth, in fluidity – in freedom, in the sense that the dancers are free, barely touching as they pass, but partners in the same pattern.

ANNE MORROW LINDBERGH (1906–2001)

Trust

Oh we've got to trust
one another again
in some essentials.

Not the narrow little
bargaining trust
that says; I'm for you
if you'll be for me.

But a bigger trust,
a trust of the sun
that does not bother
about moth and rust,
and we see it shining
in one another.

Oh don't you trust me,
don't burden me
with your life and affairs;
don't thrust me
into your cares.

But I think you may trust
the sun in me
that glows with just
as much glow as you see
in me, and no more.

But if it warms
your heart's quick core
why then trust it, it forms
one faithfulness more.

And be, oh be
a sun to me,
not a weary, insistent
personality

but a sun that shines
and goes dark, but shines
again and entwines
with the sunshine in me

till we both of us
are more glorious
and more sunny.

D. H. Lawrence (1885–1930)

In Defence of Adultery

We don't fall in love: it rises through us
the way that certain music does –
whether a symphony or ballad –
and it is sepia-coloured,
like spilt tea that inches up
the tiny tube-like gaps inside
a cube of sugar lying by a cup.
Yes, love's like that: just when we least
needed or expected it
a part of us dips into it
by chance or mishap and it seeps
through our capillaries, it clings
inside the chambers of the heart.
We're victims, we say: mere vessels,
drinking the vanilla scent
of this one's skin, the lustre
of another's eyes so skilfully
darkened with bistre. And whatever
damage might result we're not
to blame for it: love is an autocrat
and won't be disobeyed.
Sometimes we manage
to convince ourselves of that.

JULIA COPUS (1969–)

A Loyal Wife

My lord, I am grateful for these two pearls you offer me. I tremble
with uncertainty. What shall I say? I say to you . . . I am married
and have sworn to be faithful to my husband.

Perhaps you do not know that the colors of my family hang in the
Royal Park? Perhaps you do not know that my husband is honorary
lancer in the Emperor's Palace?

I think you are sincere; I think you are honorable. Therefore I have
put your pearls against my robe, and looked at them, and smiled. But
take them now again. Perhaps you will take these two tears as well?

TCHANG TSI (c. AD 800)

Troy, We Do Much Envy

Constant Penelope sends to thee, careless Ulysses.
Write not again, but come, sweet mate, thy self to revive me.
Troy we do much envy, we desolate lost ladies of Greece,
Not Priamus, nor yet all Troy can us recompense make.
O that he had, when he first took shipping to Lacedaemon,
That adulter I mean, had been o'erwhelmed with waters.
Then I had not lain now all alone, thus quivering for cold,
Nor used this complaint, nor have thought the day to be so long.

OVID (43 BC–AD 17)

from The Unquiet Grave

The greatest charm of marriage, in fact that which tenders it irresistible to those who have once tasted it, is the duologue, the permanent conversation between two people who talk over everything and everyone till death breaks the record.

CYRIL CONNOLLY (1903–74)

The Dance

I would have each couple turn,
join and unjoin, be lost
in the greater turning
of other couples, woven
in the circle of a dance,
the song of long time flowing

over them, so they may return,
turn again, in to themselves
out of desire greater than their own,
belonging to all, to each,
to the dance, and to the song
that moves them through the night.

What is fidelity? To what
does it hold? The point
of departure, or the turning road
that is departure and absence
and the way home? What we are
and what we were once

are far estranged. For those
who would not change, time
is infidelity. But we are married
until death, and are betrothed
to change. By silence, so,
I learn my song. I earn

my sunny fields by absence, once
and to come. And I love you
as I love the dance that brings you
out of the multitude
in which you come and go.
Love changes, and in change is true.

WENDELL BERRY (1934–)

Lack of Friendship

It is not lack of love, but a lack of friendship that makes unhappy marriages.

FRIEDRICH NIETZSCHE (1844–1900)

from Othello

ACT III, SCENE III

Beware . . . of jealousy!
It is the green-eyed monster, which doth mock
The meat it feeds on.

WILLIAM SHAKESPEARE (1564–1616)

from Two Noble Kinsmen

I saw her first.

WILLIAM SHAKESPEARE (attrib.) (1564–1616)

Overlap

If you made a list of the reasons why any couple got married, and another list of the reasons for their divorce, you'd have a hell of a lot of overlapping.

MIGNON MCLAUGHLIN (1913–83)

from A Short History of Tractors in Ukrainian

As Romeo and Juliet found to their cost, marriage is never just about two people falling in love, it is about families.

Marina Lewycka

Opposites Attract

Opposites attract, but after marriage, opposites attack. Most of the time, we are attracted to people who don't have the things that we have. Incompatibility is why we get married, but it's also used as a reason to divorce. Incompatibility is just a lack of communication. If we just try to love the way we want to be loved, we are in trouble. Unless you communicate, it's difficult to know how to love another person.

Dr Charles Lowery

What Counts

What counts in making a happy marriage is not so much how compatible you are, but how you deal with incompatibility.

Leo Tolstoy (1828-1910)

Change

People change and forget to tell each other.

LILLIAN HELLMAN (1907–84)

Revived Love

New love is the brightest, and long love is the greatest; but revived love is the tenderest thing on earth.

THOMAS HARDY (1840–1928)

Lasting Love

Wedding Anniversaries

1st	Cotton
2nd	Paper
3rd	Leather
4th	Flower
5th	Wood
6th	Iron
7th	Wool
8th	Bronze
9th	Copper
10th	Tin
11th	Steel
12th	Silk
13th	Lace
15th	Crystal
20th	China
25th	Silver
30th	Pearl
35th	Coral
40th	Ruby
45th	Sapphire
50th	Golden
55th	Emerald
60th	Diamond

It Takes Years to Marry

It takes years to marry completely two hearts, even of the most loving and well assorted. A happy wedlock is a long falling in love. Young persons think love belongs only to the brown-haired and crimson-cheeked. So it does for its beginning. But the golden marriage is a part of love which the Bridal day knows nothing of . . .

Such a large and sweet fruit is a complete marriage that it needs a long summer to ripen in, and then a long winter to mellow and season it. But a really happy marriage of love and judgment between a noble man and woman is one of the things so very handsome that if the sun were, as the Greeks once fabled, a god he might stop the world and hold it still now and then in order to look all day long on some example thereof, and feast his eyes on such a spectacle.

THEODORE PARKER (1810–60)

The Anniversarie

All Kings, and all their favourites,
  All glory of honours, beauties, wits,
The sun itself, which makes times, as they pass,
Is elder by a year now than it was
When thou and I first one another saw:
All other things to their destruction draw,
  Only our love hath no decay;
This no tomorrow hath, nor yesterday,
Running it never runs from us away,
But truly keeps his first, last, everlasting day.

Two graves must hide thine and my corse;
  If one might, death were no divorce.
Alas, as well as other Princes, we
(Who Prince enough in one another be)
Must leave at last in death these eye and ears,
Oft fed with true oaths, and with sweet salt tears;
  But souls where nothing dwells but love
(All other thoughts being inmates) then shall prove
This, or a love increased there above,
When bodies to their graves, souls from their graves remove.

And then we shall be thoroughly blessed;
  But we no more than all the rest.
Here upon earth we're Kings, and none but we
Can be such Kings, nor of such subjects be;
Who is so safe as we? where none can do
Treason to us, except one of us two.
  True and false fears let us refrain;
Let us love nobly, and live, and add again
Years and years unto years, till we attain
To write threescore: this is the second of our reign.

JOHN DONNE (1572–1631)

Idleness

I keep the rustic gate closed
For fear somebody might step
On the green moss. The sun grows
Warmer. You can tell it's Spring.
Once in a while, when the breeze
Shifts, I can hear the sounds of the
Village. My wife is reading
The classics. Now and then she
Asks me the meaning of a word.
I call for wine and my son
Fills my cup till it runs over.
I have only a little
Garden, but it is planted
With yellow and purple plums.

LU YU (*c.* 1200)

from Everything to Lose

May 4th 1948: I quite often look back at the pleasures and pains of youth – love, jealousy, recklessness, vanity – without forgetting their spell but no longer desiring them; while middle-aged ones like music, places, botany, conversation seem to be just as enjoyable as those wilder ones, in which there was usually some potential anguish lying in wait, like a bee in a flower. I hope there may be further surprises in store, and on the whole do not fear the advance into age . . .

May 5th: Ralph to London to the dentist. I have sprained my ankle so cannot go with him, but as the years pass I *hate* being parted from him even for an hour or so; I feel only half a person by myself, with one arm, one leg and half a face.

Warmer, softer, sweeter day: the birds sing very loudly and the pollarded trees on the road to Hungerford station seem to be holding little bunches of greenery in their fists.

FRANCES PARTRIDGE (1900–2002)

from The Velveteen Rabbit

BEING LOVED

What is REAL?' asked the Rabbit one day, when they were lying side by side near the nursery fender, before Nana came to tidy the room. 'Does it mean having things that buzz inside you and a stick-out handle?'

'Real isn't how you are made,' said the Skin Horse. 'It's a thing that happens to you. When someone loves you for a long, long time, not just to play with, but REALLY loves you, then you become Real.'

'Does it hurt?' asked the Rabbit.

'Sometimes,' said the Skin Horse, for he was always truthful. 'When you are Real you don't mind being hurt.'

'Does it happen all at once, like being wound up,' he asked, 'or bit by bit?'

'It doesn't happen all at once,' said the Skin Horse. 'You become. It takes a long time. That's why it doesn't happen often to people who break easily, or have sharp edges, or who have to be carefully kept. Generally, by the time you are Real, most of your hair has been loved off, and your eyes drop out and you get loose in your joints and very shabby. But these things don't matter at all, because once you are Real you can't be ugly, except to people who don't understand.'

'I suppose you are real?' said the Rabbit. And then he wished he had not said it, for he thought the Skin Horse might be sensitive. But the Skin Horse only smiled.

'Someone made me Real,' he said. 'That was a great many years ago; but once you are Real you can't become unreal again. It lasts for always.'

MARGERY WILLIAMS (1881–1944)

Cancer

Her sumptuous legs, promising so much,
Arresting other men's eyes to their appraisal
Kept me awake at night with hot imagining
Made me cry out from voluptuous dreams
Until one night she allowed my hand
To stroke them kindly and make them mine.

Her arms were branches from the same tree
Stretching long and luscious from the same trunk.
I could blow my way up and down this downy surface
Like a tender zephyr
Bending down a thousand brown shoots
Before they sprang up straight again.

Now her arms are become twigs.
No longer concealed by those soft curves
Bones life never allowed me to see
Have disclosed the scaffold that was always waiting there
Her skin glows no more
Even the hairs do not bend to the breath.

Now the steroids swelling up her legs
Have made her flesh weep water
Enough to wet the carpet and my eyes.
But when I rub her thin thighs with oil of lavender,
Left to my own appraisal I love her more.
Behind the bones, alongside crumpled skin
The same large brown eyes, larger now, shine out
As brightly as 35 years ago
When our souls first were joined together.

MICHAEL YOUNG (1915–2002)

from The Year of Magical Thinking

Marriage is memory, marriage is time. 'She didn't know the songs,' I recall being told that a friend of a friend had said after an attempt to repeat the experience. Marriage is not only time: it is also, paradoxically, a denial of time. For 40 years I saw myself through John's eyes. I did not age. This year for the first time since I was 29 I saw myself through the eyes of others.

JOAN DIDION (1934–)

Those Who Love Deeply

Those who love deeply never grow old.

ARTHUR WING PINERO (1855–1934)

To Jenny, 1856

My heart's beloved

I am writing you again, because I am alone and because it troubles me always to have a dialogue with you in my head, without your knowing anything about it or hearing it or being able to answer . . . You have only to be snatched away from me even in a mere dream, and I know immediately that the time has only served, as do sun and rain for plants, for growth. The moment you are absent, my love for you shows itself to be what it is, a giant, in which are crowded together all the energy of my spirit and all the character of my heart . . .

There are actually many females in the world, and some among them are beautiful. But where could I find again a face, whose every feature, even every wrinkle, is a reminder of the greatest and sweetest memories of my life? Even my endless pains, my irreplaceable losses I read in your sweet countenance, and I kiss away the pain when I kiss your sweet face. 'Buried in her arms, awakened by her kisses' – namely, in your arms and by your kisses, and I grant the Brahmins and Pythagoras their doctrine of regeneration and Christianity its doctrine of resurrection . . . Goodbye, my sweet heart. I kiss you and the children many thousand times.

Yours,
Karl

KARL MARX (1818–1983)

from the Chinese 'She King'

Says the wife, 'It is cock-crow'
Says the husband, 'It is grey dawn'
'Rise, Sir, and look at the night –
If the morning star be not shining.
Bestir yourself, and move about,
To shoot the wild ducks and geese.

'When your arrows and line have found them,
I will dress them fitly for you.
When they are dressed, we will drink (together over them),
And I will hope to grow old with you.
Your lute in your hands
Will emit its quiet pleasant tones.

'When I know those whose acquaintance you wish,
I will give them of the ornaments of my girdle.
When I know those with whom you are cordial,
I will send to them the ornaments of my girdle.
When I know those whom you love,
I will repay their friendship from the ornaments of my girdle.'

(Trans. James Legge 1815–97)
from the world's oldest book of poetry, the 'She King'

Divorce

I always knew
I ought to get a divorce
Everyone has them
How can I be a paid-up member
Of the modern movement
Married thirty years to the same man

I would have looked so good
On the witness stand
In an elegant understated outfit
My hand on the Bible
The only sticky bit
Would be going home
Without you

ANONYMOUS

Being Boring

'May you live in interesting times.' Chinese curse

If you ask me 'What's new?', I have nothing to say
Except that the garden is growing.
I had a slight cold but it's better today.
I'm content with the way things are going.
Yes, he is the same as he usually is,
Still eating and sleeping and snoring.
I get on with my work. He gets on with his.
I know this is all very boring.

There was drama enough in my turbulent past:
Tears and passion – I've used up a tankful.
No news is good news, and long may it last,
If nothing much happens, I'm thankful.
A happier cabbage you never did see,
My vegetable spirits are soaring.
If you're after excitement, steer well clear of me.
I want to go on being boring.

I don't go to parties. Well, what are they for,
If you don't need to find a new lover?
You drink and you listen and drink a bit more
And you take the next day to recover.
Someone to stay home with was all my desire
And, now that I've found a safe mooring,
I've just one ambition in life: I aspire
To go on and on being boring

WENDY COPE (1945–)

from Love in the Time of Cholera

She clung to her husband. And it was just at the time when he needed her most, because he suffered the disadvantage of being ten years ahead of her as he stumbled alone through the mists of old age, with the even greater disadvantage of being a man and weaker than she was. In the end they knew each other so well that by the time they had been married for thirty years they were like a single divided being, and they felt uncomfortable at the frequency with which they guessed each other's thoughts without intending to, or the ridiculous accident of one of them anticipating in public what the other was going to say. Together they had overcome the daily incomprehension, the instantaneous hatred, the reciprocal nastiness and fabulous flashes of glory in the conjugal conspiracy. It was the time when they loved each other best, without hurry or excess, when both were most conscious of and grateful for their incredible victories over adversity. Life would still present them with other mortal trials, of course, but that no longer mattered: they were on the other shore.

GABRIEL GARCÍA MÁRQUEZ (1928–)

To His Wife on the Fourteenth
Anniversary of Her Wedding-Day, With a Ring

'Thee, Mary, with this ring I wed,'
So, fourteen years ago, I said.
Behold another ring! 'For what?'
To wed thee o'er again – why not?

With that first ring I married youth,
Grace, beauty, innocence, and truth;
Taste long admired, sense long revered,
And all my Molly then appeared.

If she, by merit since disclosed,
Prove twice the woman I supposed,
I plead that double merit now,
To justify a double vow.

Here then, today, – with faith as sure,
With ardour as intense and pure,
As when amidst the rites divine
I took thy troth, and plighted mine, –
To thee, sweet girl, my second ring,
A token, and a pledge, I bring;
With this I wed, till death us part,
Thy riper virtues to my heart;
Those virtues which, before untried,
The wife has added to the bride –
Those virtues, whose progressive claim,
Endearing wedlock's very name,
My soul enjoys, my song approves,
For conscience' sake as well as love's.

For why? – They show me every hour
Honour's high thought, affection's power,
Discretion's deed, sound judgment's sentence,
And teach me all things – but repentance.

SAMUEL BISHOP (1731–95)

Wrong Turnings

So we go back, driving through the clear light,
The fields spread out, birds scuttering upwards
And on the way from London we took wrong turnings,
Missed signs, found ourselves forced off the right way
By large ugly trucks, but all the time you know,
You and I, we've been going the right way,
And eventually we were there, the light leaping
Off the sea as we crossed through the farm,
And saw the stables, the horses better kept now,
Time improving not taking away and
Time has taken nothing from us; only
Given, over and over, and here we are again
In one of our old haunts, you in your grand raincoat,
Me, with too many coats and boots and things, as usual,
Climbing out into our past, visiting
The old house where we came with our first child
At the edge of the ocean, a place
Of mud and creeks and changing currents
Where machinery from old gravel pits
Lies swathed in seaweed, basking in the mud,
A wooden boat entirely covered in slime
Lies in the creek, the water trickling by
And we wonder if that was our boat,
The one which drifted past us and we kept
Then one day it drifted away
And we never found it, but our house
Had gone, the little wooden shack with a deck
From where we used to catch crabs
Then throw them back,
In its stead was a brick building,
Uglier yes, but sturdier, and the man
Who lived there now was very sick,

And when there were storms turned his chair to face the storm.
This is the place at the very edge
Where the wind whips and water rises,
Beyond the sea wall, and we've been there,
Baby, beyond the sea wall, where
Things change any moment, every moment,
But if you hang on tight it's okay
Though the roof blows off, the creek erodes,
We're still there, and you carried
Anna high on your shoulders when
She was tired, her curls in the wind,
Little red Wellingtons, and you were
Strong and young and whenever you went out
In your boat, you got it stuck and came back
Dragging it, always getting stuck and getting
Lost, but we made it all the same,
And here our place as it had always been,
Treacherous, playful, a sanctuary for birds.
Every few steps a plover flew up, or a gull,
Skidding over the grey merciless sea
And we walked and walked,
To broken bridges and the empty beach
Flung out before us, all ours,
And we walked too far, and missed
The turning, but we never really missed it
Because all the time we were together
And all the wrong and right turnings
Lead only to each other, you with
Anna on your shoulders, two mops of curly hair,
Wellington-booted pair, returning from
A walk which went wrong somehow.
And me, restless I know, neither
Quite in or out of an experience
Always watching, on a seesaw between
Past and future, only intermittingly balanced in the present,
And when we stop to take a breath

You are looking up at the birds in the sky
While I look down at a tiny spider clambering in the sea lavender
Looking in different directions from the same place,
We have at times turned our chairs to the thunder.
You and I, through the years, through the years,
Sausages cooked by the fire, wind lashing the window,
And all the wrong and right turnings
Leading only to each other,
To this moment now.

SALLY EMERSON

Love Poem

As I sat at my old desk, writing
in golden evening sunshine,
my wife came in suddenly
and, standing beside me.
said, 'I love you'
(this year she will be sixty-three and I shall be sixty-eight)
Then I looked at her and saw
not the grey-haired woman but the girl I married in 1922:
poetry shining through that faithful prose,
a fresh flower in bloom.
I said, 'You are a rose'
(Thinking how awful it would have been if I had missed her)
and I kissed her.

VIVIAN DE SOLA PINTO (1895–1969)

A Valediction: Forbidding Mourning

As virtuous men pass mildly away,
    And whisper to their souls, to go,
Whilst some of their sad friends do say,
    The breath goes now, and some say, no:

So let us melt, and make no noise,
    No tear-floods, nor sigh-tempests move,
'Twere profanation of our joys
    To tell the laity our love.

Moving of th'earth brings harms and fears,
    Men reckon what it did and meant,
But trepidation of the spheres,
    Though greater far, is innocent.

Dull sublunary lovers' love
    (Whose soul is sense) cannot admit
Absence, because it doth remove
    Those things which elemented it.

But we by a love, so much refined,
    That our selves know not what it is,
Inter-assurèd of the mind,
    Care less, eyes, lips, and hands to miss.

Our two souls therefore, which are one,
    Though I must go, endure not yet
A breach, but an expansion,
    Like gold to aery thinness beat.

If they be two, they are two so
    As stiff twin compasses are two,
Thy soul the fixed foot, makes no show
    To move, but doth, if th'other do.

And though it in the centre sit,
    Yet when the other far doth roam,
It leans, and hearkens after it,
    And grows erect, as that comes home.

Such wilt thou be to me, who must
    Like th'other foot, obliquely run;
Thy firmness draws my circle just,
    And makes me end, where I begun.

JOHN DONNE (1572–1631)

Marriage Is One Long Conversation

Marriage is one long conversation, chequered by disputes. The disputes are valueless; they but ingrain the difference; the heroic heart of woman prompting her at once to nail her colours to the mast. But in the intervals, almost unconsciously, and with no desire to shine, the whole material of life is turned over and over, ideas are struck out and shared, the two persons more and more adapt their notions one to suit the other, and in the process of time, without sound of trumpet, they conduct each other into new worlds of thought.

ROBERT LOUIS STEVENSON (1850–94)

Joined for Life

What greater thing is there for two human souls than to feel that they are joined for life – to strengthen each other in all labour, to rest on each other in all sorrow, to minister to each other in all pain, to be with each other in silent, unspeakable memories at the moment of the last parting.

GEORGE ELIOT (1819–80)

Isolation

Lovers are temporarily free from the burden of isolation that every individual bears.

SHULAMITH FIRESTONE (1945–)

Same Direction

Love does not consist in gazing at each other but in looking together in the same direction.

ANTOINE DE SAINT-EXUPÉRY (1900–44)

Marrying at Sixty-Six for the First Time

Being married is like having somebody permanently in your corner; it feels limitless, not limited.

GLORIA STEINEM (1934–)

A Continuous Central Life

Campaigners against [marriage], from Shelley and the Mills on, have been remarkably crass in posing the simple dilemma, 'either you want to stay together or you don't – if you do, you need not promise; if you don't, you ought to part.' This ignores the chances of inner conflict, and the deep human need for a continuous central life that lasts through genuine, but passing, changes of mood. The need to be able to rely on other people is not some sort of shameful weakness; it is an aspect of the need to be true to oneself.

MARY MIDGLEY (1919–)

What You've Been Through

A lady of forty-seven who has been married 27 years and has six children knows what love really is and once described it for me like this: 'Love is what you've been through with someone'.

JAMES THURBER (1894–1961)

Grow Old Along With Me

Grow old along with me!
The best is yet to be.

ROBERT BROWNING (1812–89)

His Late Wife's Wedding-Ring

The ring so worn, as you behold,
So thin, so pale, is yet of gold:
The passion such it was to prove,
Worn with life's cares, love yet was love.

GEORGE CRABBE (1754–1832)

The Only Meaning

There is a land of the living and a land of the dead, and the bridge is love, the only survival, the only meaning.

THORNTON WILDER (1897–1975)

Late Fragment

And did you get what
you wanted from this life, even so?
I did.
And what did you want?
To call myself beloved, to feel myself
beloved on the earth.

RAYMOND CARVER (1939–88)

ACKNOWLEDGEMENTS

Many thanks to all those who have offered suggestions and support, including Amanda Craig, Valerie Grove, Canon David Meara of St Bride's, Fleet Street, Bel Mooney, Rosemary Squire, Cita and Irwin Stelzer, Michael and Anna Stothard, David Tang. Thanks also to Jill Foulston, Connie Robertson and Vivien Redman.

The publishers would like to acknowledge the following for permission to reproduce copyright material:

Extracts from *The Authorized Version of The Bible* (*The King James Bible*), the rights of which are vested in the Crown, are reproduced by permission of the Crown's Patentee, Cambridge University Press.

Extracts from 'The Song of Solomon' in *The Revised Standard Version of the Bible,* reprinted by permission of the National Council of Churches of Christ in the USA.

Dannie Abse: 'Epithalamion' from *New and Collected Poems* (Hutchinson, 2003), copyright © Dannie Abse 2003, reprinted by permission of PFD (www.pfd.co.uk) on behalf of the author.

Diane Ackerman: from *A Natural History of Love* (Vintage 1994), reprinted by permission of Random House, Inc.

Daisy Ashford: from *The Young Visiters* (Chatto & Windus, 1920), reprinted by permission of The Random House Group Ltd.

Margaret Atwood: 'Variation on the Word Sleep' from *Poems 1976–1986* (Virago, 1992), reprinted by permission of the publishers, Little, Brown Book Group UK.

W. H. Auden: 'Twelve Songs XII: Some Say That Love's a Little Boy' from *Collected Shorter Poems 1927–1957* (Faber, 1966), reprinted by permission of the publishers, Faber & Faber Ltd.

Pam Ayres: 'Yes, I'll Marry You, My Dear' from *With These Hands* (Weidenfeld & Nicolson, 1997), copyright © Pam Ayres 1997, reprinted by permission of Sheil Land Associates on behalf of the author.

Charles Baudelaire: 'Jewels' from *Les Fleurs Du Mal* translated by Alan Conder (Cassell, 1952), reprinted by permission of the publisher, a division of The Orion Publishing Group.

Louis de Bernières: extract from *Captain Corelli's Mandolin* (Secker & Warburg, 1994), reprinted by permission of the Random House Group Ltd.

Wendell Berry: 'The Dance' from *Collected Poems 1952–1982* (North Point Press, 1985), copyright © 1985 by Wendell Berry, reprinted by permission of North Point Press. a division of Farrar, Straus & Giroux LLC.

John Betjeman: 'In a Bath Teashop' and 'A Subaltern's Love-Song' from *Collected Poems* (John Murray, 2001), reprinted by permission of the publisher.

Elizabeth Bishop: 'Close close all night …' *from Edgar Allen Poe and the Juke Box: Uncollected Poems, Drafts & Fragments* edited by Alice Quinn (Farrar, Straus & Giroux, 2006), reprinted by permission of Farrar, Straus & Giroux, LLC.

Stephen Bishop: 'Looking for the Right One', words and music by Stephen Bishop, copyright © 1978 Justin Case Music Publishing Company, Universal/MCA Music Ltd, lyrics reprinted by permission of Music Sales Ltd. All rights reserved. International copyright secured.

Michael Blumenthal: 'A Marriage' from *Against Romance* (Pleasure Boat Studio, 2006), reprinted by permission of Pleasure Boat Studio: A Literary Press.

Napoleon Bonaparte: letter to Josephine Beauharnais translated by Christine Czechowski in *Love Letters* edited by Antonia Fraser (Weidenfeld & Nicolson, 1976) reprinted by permission of the publisher, a division of The Orion Publishing Group.

Raymond Carver: 'Late Fragment' from *All of Us: The Collected Poems* (The Harvill Press, 1996), copyright © Raymond Carver 1996, reprinted by permission of The Random House Group Ltd and International Creative Management, Inc.

Nina Cassian: 'Temptation' translated by Brenda Walker and Andrea Deletant from *Nina Cassian: Life Sentence* edited by William Jay Smith (Anvil, 1990), copyright © Nina Cassian 1990, reprinted by permission of the publishers, Anvil Press Poetry and W. W. Norton & Company.

Kate Clanchy: 'For a Wedding' from *Slattern* (Macmillan, 1995), reprinted by permission of Macmillan, London, UK.

John Clare: 'First Love' and from 'To Mary' both from *John Clare: The Oxford Authors* edited by Eric Robinson and David Powell (OUP, 1984), copyright © Eric Robinson 1984, reprinted by permission of Curtis Brown Group Ltd, London, on behalf of Eric Robinson.

Eddie Cooley: [see John Davenport]

Cyril Connolly: from *The Unquiet Grave* (Hamish Hamilton, 1945), copyright © Cyril Connolly 1944, reprinted by permission of the author c/o Rogers, Coleridge & White Ltd, 20 Powis Mews, London WII IJN.

Duff Cooper: letter to Diana Manners from Artemis Cooper: *A Durable Fire: The Letters of Duff and Diana 1913–1930* (Collins, 1983), reprinted by permission of Artemis Cooper.

Wendy Cope: 'Valentine' and 'As Sweet' from *Serious Concerns* (Faber, 1991). 'Being Boring' from *If I Don't Know* (Faber, 2001), reprinted by permission of the publishers, Faber & Faber Ltd.

Julia Copus: 'In Defence of Adultery' from *In Defence of Adultery* (Bloodaxe Books, 2002), reprinted by permission of the publishers.

Gregory Corso: from 'Marriage', reprinted by permission of Sheri Baird, executor of the Corso Estate.

Robert Creeley: 'Love Comes Quietly' from *The Collected Poems of Robert Creeley 1945–1975* (University of California Press, 1982), reprinted by permission of Marion Boyars Publishers Ltd.

Louise Cuddon: 'I'll Be There', copyright © Louise Cuddon 2004, first published in *Poems and Readings for Weddings* edited by Julia Watson (Penguin, 2004), reprinted by permission of Jonathan Clowes Ltd.

E. E. Cummings: 'i carry your heart with me' from *Complete Poems 1904–1962* edited by George J. Firmage, copyright © 1991 by the Trustees for the E E Cummings Trust and George J. Firmage, reprinted by permission of W. W. Norton & Company.

Daily Mail article: 'How passion gives way to cuddles within two years', *Daily Mail,* 1 February 2006, reprinted by permission of Solo Syndication.

John Davenport & Eddie Cooley: 'Fever', copyright © 1956 Fort Knox Music Inc and Trio Music Co, copyright renewed, lyrics

U. A. Fanthorpe: 'Atlas' from *Collected Poems 1978–2003* (Peterloo Poets, 2005), copyright © U. A. Fanthorpe 2005, reprinted by permission of the publishers.

James Fenton: 'In Paris with You' from *Selected Poems* (Penguin. 2006), copyright © James Fenton 2006, reprinted by permission of PFD (www.pfd.co.uk) on behalf of James Fenton.

Lawrence Ferlinghetti: translation of Jacques Prevert: 'Alicante' from *Selections from Paroles* (Penguin, 1965) English translation copyright © Lawrence Ferlinghetti 1965, reprinted by permission of Pollinger Ltd and the proprietor.

F. Scott Fitzgerald written as Thomas Parke D'Invilliers: Epigraph to *The Great Gatsby* (Penguin, 2000), reprinted by permission of David Higham Associates.

Zelda Fitzgerald: extract from a letter from *Dear Scott, Dearest Zelda: The Love Letters of F. Scott and Zelda Fitzgerald* edited by Jackson R. Bryer and Cathy W. Barks (Bloomsbury, 2002), reprinted by permission of David Higham Associates

John Fuller: 'Valentine' from *Collected Poems* (Chatto & Windus, 1996), copyright John Fuller 1996, reprinted by permission of PFD (www.pfd.co.uk) on behalf of John Fuller.

Robert Graves: 'Symptoms of Love' and 'A Slice of Wedding Cake' from *Complete Poems* (Carcanet, 1999), reprinted by permission of the publishers, Carcanet Press Ltd.

Lorenz Hart: 'I Wish I Were in Love Again' from *Babes in Arms*, words by Lorenz Hart, copyright © 1937 (renewed) Chappell & Co & Williamson Music, Inc. All rights administered by Warner/Chappell Music Ltd, London W6 8BS; lyrics reprinted with their permission.

A. P. Herbert: from 'Why Doesn't She Come?' from *She-Shanties*

(1926), reprinted by permission of A. P. Watt Ltd on behalf of the Executors of the Estate of Jocelyn Herbert, M. T. Perkins and Polly M. V. R. Perkins.

Jane Holland: 'They are a Tableau Kissing at the Gate' from *The Brief History of Disreputable Woman* (Bloodaxe Books, 1997), reprinted by permission of the publishers.

Miroslav Holub: 'Love' translated by Ian Milner from *Miroslav Holub: Poems Before and After: Collected English Translations* (Bloodaxe Books, 1990), reprinted by permission of the publishers.

Michael Ignatieff: from 'Lodged in the Heart and Memory', reprinted by permission of A. P. Watt Ltd on behalf of Michael Ignatieff.

Elizabeth Jennings: 'Years Ago' from *Collected Poems* (Carcanet, 1986), reprinted by permission of David Higham Associates

Brian Jones: 'Husband to Wife: Party Going' from *Freeborn John* (Carcanet, 1990), reprinted by permission of the publishers, Carcanet Press Ltd.

T. Harri Jones: 'A Birthday Poem for Madeleine' from *The Collected Poems of T. Harri Jones* (Gomer Press, 1977), reprinted by permission of the publisher.

Jenny Joseph: 'The Sun Has Burst the Sky' from *Selected Poems* (Bloodaxe, 1992), copyright © Jenny Joseph 1992, reprinted by permission of Johnson & Alcock Ltd.

Jean Kenward: 'Stepmother', copyright © Jean Kenward, reprinted by permission of the author.

Philip Larkin: 'Is It For Now or For Always?' from *Collected Poems* (Faber, 1988), reprinted by permission of the publishers, Faber & Faber Ltd.

James Thurber: 'What You've Been Through', reprinted by permission of the Barbara Hogensen Agency Inc.

C. K. Williams: 'Love: Beginnings' from *New and Selected Poems* (Bloodaxe Books, 1995) reprinted by permission of the publishers, Bloodaxe Books and Farrar, Straus & Giroux, LLC.

P. G. Wodehouse: from *Jeeves in the Offing* (Herbert Jenkins, 1960) and from *Chumps Make the Best Husbands* (Herbert Jenkins, 1922), reprinted by permission of The Random House Group Ltd.

Virginia Woolf: published in G. Spater and I. Parsons: *A Marriage of True Minds: an Intimate Portrait of Leonard and Virginia Woolf* (Jonathan Cape, 1977), reprinted by permission of The Society of Authors, as the Literary Representatives of the Estate of Virginia Woolf.

W. B. Yeats: 'He Wishes for the Cloths of Heaven' from *The Collected Poems of W. B. Yeats* (1983), reprinted by permission of A. P. Watt Ltd on behalf of Michael B. Yeats .

Lu Yu: 'Idleness', translated by Kenneth Rexroth from *One Hundred Poems from the Chinese* (New Directions, 1971), copyright © Kenneth Rexroth 1971, reprinted by permission of New Directions Publishing Corp.

Although we have tried to trace and contact all copyright holders before publication, this has not been possible in every case. If notified, the publisher will be pleased to rectify any errors or omissions at the earliest opportunity.

Index of First Lines

INDEX OF AUTHORS

IN LOVING MEMORY

Edited by Sally Emerson

In Loving Memory is a new collection of poetry and writing on that most difficult of subjects: the death of someone dear to us. Selected by the author Sally Emerson, this wide-ranging anthology offers a wealth of suggestions for funerals and memorial services, as well as poems to offer comfort, support and peace of mind.

The sections in this collection focus on the many emotions that a death can bring: there are poems that deal with grief and rage, parting and remembering, thanksgiving and finding peace. Here too are poems of inspiration, some that celebrate the power of love, and others that simply say goodbye. Included are selections from the Bible and *The Prophet*, much loved poets such as Tennyson, Wordsworth and Blake, as well as more recent works: excerpts from *Captain Corelli's Mandolin*, for example, and Auden's 'Funeral Blues', famously used in *Four Weddings and a Funeral*.

As the range of material in this collection shows, it is poetry to which we turn in times of grief that best encapsulates our feelings and emotions. And whether you are looking for solace or understanding, reminiscing or moving on, this anthology will offer words of help to match your mood.

A Little, Brown Original
ISBN 978-0-316-72599-6